FROM PATMOS
TO THE BARRIO

subverting imperial myths

FROM PATMOS
TO THE BARRIO

subverting imperial myths

DAVID A. SÁNCHEZ

FORTRESS PRESS
Minneapolis

For
Denna Marie
Isabella Loren
and
Mayali Belen

FROM PATMOS TO THE BARRIO
The Subversion of Imperial Myths from the Book of Revelation to Today

Cover image: Copyright © 2008 CORBIS. Used by permission
Cover design: Kevin van der Leek Design
Book design: Eileen Z. Engebretson

This book was typeset using Minion Pro, Lithos, and Mesquite Std.

Library of Congress Cataloging-in-Publication Data
Sánchez, David Arthur, 1960–
  From Patmos to the barrio : the subversion of imperial myths from the book of Revelation to the present / by David Arthur Sánchez.
     p. cm.
  Includes bibliographical references and index.
  ISBN-13: 978-0-8006-6260-8 (alk. paper)
  ISBN-13: 978-0-8006-6259-2 (alk. paper)
  1. Bible. N.T. Revelation XII—Criticism, interpretation, etc. 2. Bible. N.T. Revelation XII—Postcolonial criticism. 3. Hispanic American theology. I. Title.
  BS2825.52.S26 2008
  228'.064—dc22   2007048214

The paper used in this publication meets the minimum requirements of American National Standard for Information Sciences—Permanence of Paper for Printed Library Materials, ANSI Z329.48-1984.

Manufactured in the U.S.A.

12   11   10   09   08   1   2   3   4   5   6   7   8   9   10

CONTENTS

PREFACE

In the winter of 1999, while engaged in a graduate research project entitled African Americans and the Bible, I received my first exposure to the evaluation of ethno-religious performances of the Bible. By Biblical performances, I refer to those modern expressions of Biblical interpretation as manifested in both religious and cultural representations (that is, art, spoken-word, dance, song, sermon, architecture, and so on). This performance-centric re-orientation represented a personal moment of methodological destabilization, especially when contrasted to my previous text-centric training. The fruit of this destabilization, however, was the self-realization that interpretation of the Bible must incorporate the analysis of both texts and subsequent textual performances: the ancient in conversation with the modern and vice-versa.

My contribution to the research project was the analysis of the public art or murals located on 125th Street in Harlem, New York. What I discovered was that a people, African Americans, articulated a unique socio-cultural understanding of that collection of texts we call the Bible. Biblical themes such as imperialism, human bondage, marginalization, exile, exodus, and freedom of the human spirit abounded. African American theologians and political philosophers who preached and taught these themes—albeit from radically different perspectives—were also prevalent in the Harlem murals: Martin Luther King Jr., Malcolm X, Marcus Garvey, and Frederick Douglass, to name a representative few. It was, in my estimation, a finely tuned demonstration of a unique brand of Biblical interpretation directly related to and resultant from the specific socio-cultural location of the modern interpreter(s).

As a result of this experience I began to reflect on my own cultural location. As a citizen of the United States of Mexican ancestry, I began to ponder the public religious and cultural representations from whence

I came and began to ask whether the methodological skills I honed in Harlem were transferable and relevant to my world: East Los Angeles, where I was born and raised. Immediately, my thoughts flashed back to the abundance of murals that were so much a part of my childhood landscape. Not recalling the specifics of the depictions, I made a pilgrimage back to my former neighborhood and its environs to begin a systematic analysis of our ethno-cultural and religious productions. What stood out most prominently during my ethnographic work was the omnipresence of the Mexican Virgin of Guadalupe in mural form. Her representations were so abundant it made data collection overwhelming. The barrio was saturated with her image, and it could be found on multiple venues, including liquor stores, churches, auto shops, meat markets, highway underpasses, eateries, vehicles, and so on. Wherever Mexicans or individuals of Mexican ancestry resided, she was there. What follows is an attempt to decipher the overt saturation of public images of the Virgin of Guadalupe in the barrios of East Los Angeles as public performances of a unique and socially located form of Biblical interpretation.

I owe a great deal of gratitude to Brigitte Kahl, Hal Taussig, and Jean-Pierre Ruiz for their vision, insight, unwavering support, and countless readings of this manuscript in its earliest stages. To my colleagues Jeff Siker and Matt Dillon, your thoughtful and detailed critiques of specific chapters of this manuscript were invaluable. I am also thankful for the many teachers over my graduate and professional career who challenged me to look at our common object of study, Bible, from multiple interpretive perspectives: Burton Mack, James Robinson, James Sanders, Gregory Riley, J. William Whedbee, Alan Segal, Fred Weidmann, Deirdre Good, Vincent Wimbush, and Seth Schwartz. I am also greatly indebted to the Hispanic Theological Initiative whose moral and financial support made this project possible. I would also like to thank my colleagues in the Loyola Marymount University Theological Colloquium for their thoughtful comments during the writing and editorial process of this manuscript. And finally, I would like to thank Ernest Rose, LMU's Chief Academic Officer and Michael Engh, S. J., LMU's Dean of the Bellarmine College of Liberal Arts for their encouragement and support of this project.

It has also been my privilege to have created this manuscript in venues that have been inspiring in the breadth of their collections, the dedication of their staffs, and the intellectual ambiance of their facilities: Butler Library of Columbia University; Burke Library at Union Theological Seminary, New York; Honnold Library of the Claremont Graduate School; the library at the Claremont School of Theology; Loyola Marymount's Charles Von der Ahe Library; Martin Luther King Jr. Library of California State University Los Angeles; and the Huntington Library of San Marino, California.

I would like to thank my family, Denna, Isabella, and Mayali, for their unwavering love, support, dedication, and patience and their interjections of fun and laughter throughout the process. Finally, I am grateful to my late brother, Armando Alonso Brito Jr., for encouraging me to endeavor this improbable path.

A protestor holds an iconic image of the Virgin of Guadalupe during a demonstration against U.S. immigration policies outside the White House in 2006. Copyright © AFP/Getty Images. Used by permission.

INTRODUCTION

A Touch of Patmos
in the Barrios
of East Los Angeles

To VENTURE INTO THE AREAS that compose the eastern periphery of Los Angeles is to enter a world where the collective sensibilities of a people are displayed in a very public fashion. Public art—more specifically, murals—gracefully invite both the serious and the casual onlooker to ponder the stories of a people who have not been privileged in mainstream venues such as the media, museums, the academy, or literature. These public displays represent the sub-urban hopes, fears, despair, joy, and anger of a people who would call themselves Mexicans and Chicanas/os.[1] Therefore, the walls of the barrios of East Los Angeles play the functional role of a public repository for an alternative, counter history. They serve as the intellectual and physical canvas for a collective and subversive sociopolitical identity. As a result, they are organic sites of sociopolitical resistance primarily because they challenge traditional accounts of the European colonization of the southwest United States. Therefore, at their very core, these displays are challenges to the previously constructed histories of dominant groups and, in the truest sense, postcolonial performances.

One such example of this sub-urban and subversive posturing, which is my point of departure, is the omnipresent figure of the Virgin of Guadalupe in East Los Angeles. To many on the outside, she represents a quirky symbol of a specifically Mexican brand of Roman Catholicism. To some insiders, her role is limited to the feminine representation of the divine that is so firmly embedded in ancient Mexican—and by extension, Chicana/o—religious sensibilities. But to those inclined toward a posture of resistance, the appeal to the iconography of the Virgin of Guadalupe

1

represents a subversive form of countercolonial and counterimperial resistance. Whether employed by César Chávez and the United Farm Workers union as they stood against the powerful landowners in the Southwest United States, by Emiliano Zapata and his land movement as they confronted the powerful politicos of the Mexican government, or by Miguel Hidalgo y Costilla, who initiated the revolution that would finally expel Spanish rule after almost three hundred years of occupation, the icon of the Virgin of Guadalupe and her evocative history serve as a symbol of resistance for the marginalized against the powerful. Accordingly, the Virgin of Guadalupe is ingrained in the collective psyches of Mexican and Chicana/o peoples today. One need look no further than to her public display at recent pro-immigration rallies across the United States.

The pressing question is, how did she become a locus of resistance? Or even more appropriately, how did we come to recognize her as such? To answer these questions, we need to assess two specific moments in history: (1) seventeenth-century Mexico, where the first literary depictions of the apparition of the Virgin of Guadalupe account are attested; and (2) first-century Asia Minor, specifically the island of Patmos, where John the Seer received his apocalypse and subsequently wrote the final entry of the New Testament, the book of Revelation. The first context, seventeenth-century Mexico, is obvious; this period saw the genesis of the literary component of the myth in question. But what could first-century Patmos have to do with the Virgin of Guadalupe and contemporary Mexicans and Chicanas/os? What is this "touch of Patmos in East Los Angeles" to which I allude?

This journey is best begun by simultaneously reading Revelation 12:1 while gazing at a photo of the Virgin of Guadalupe (see appendix, plate 2). Could it be that the woman described in Revelation 12 as one clothed in the sun, standing on the moon, and with a crown of twelve stars is the literary impetus for subsequent artistic representations of the Virgin of Guadalupe? If so, is there a specific motif of resistance in the book of Revelation or, more specifically, in Revelation 12 that would illuminate later appropriations of this text? I think the answer to both questions is a compelling yes.

Therefore, I take the reader back to where it all began. Surprisingly, the beginning is not colonial Mexico, where the apparition of the Virgin presumably took place on a hill just north of Mexico City in 1531. Instead, the beginning can be traced to a most unlikely location and time: a rocky, desolate island in the Aegean Sea, known in the first century C.E. as Patmos. What will emerge is a powerful relationship between an ancient Christian prophet and the subsequent literary and artistic manifestations of the Queen of Heaven in the form of the Virgin of Guadalupe.

THESIS AND ASSUMPTIONS

Throughout the course of human history, dominating peoples have used imperial myths to justify their claims to power and to subjugate those under their jurisdiction. These myths come in a variety of forms. Some claim a special relationship between a deity or deities and a people, while others draw a direct genealogical line between the gods and a monarch or a prophetic figure of the ruling class. Regardless of the form, these myths serve the ruling class as justification for the construction of a social hierarchy. In contrast, those who have been marginalized by these myths have persistently reconfigured and manipulated them. In moments of resistance, those living on the margins of power claim these imperial myths on their own interpretive terms, creating alternative categories of power in which they construct themselves as the primary beneficiaries of newly reformulated social hierarchies.

Literary and artistic representations of these complex cultural encounters and their subsequent relationships are generally obscured because it is usually those with power who document such encounters, thereby relegating strategies of the marginalized to the fringes of our collective recollections and leaving us a one-sided, unbalanced history. As recipients of these unbalanced histories, we must redirect our historical gaze to the shadows of empire, to those interstitial and hybrid spaces where marginalized peoples are actively and continually producing offstage countermythologies. Here, according to political scientist James C. Scott, the subliminal "weapons of the weak" are most palpable.[2] And as I shall demonstrate in the following chapters, the creation of these countermythologies is a perduring human phenomenon that transcends both time and culture. Whenever and wherever power is exerted, power is deflected.

It should also be emphasized that the marginalized persons' subversions of imperial mythologies are constructed in such a manner as to give the illusion of acquiescence to power, when in reality they facilitate the undermining of the very myths drawn on in their subjugation. This performance of misrepresentations is the real genius of the subversion of imperial mythologies. It is an offstage performance "that represents a critique of power spoken behind the back of the dominant,"[3] or it is encoded in such a way that even when the dominant become aware of its presence (public performance), they fail to recognize the agenda of its implicit social critique and resultant ideological reordering of power relationships.

With these assumptions in place, my thesis is that people living on the margins of power—specifically in imperial, colonial, and neocolonial contexts—will challenge the centers of power in patterned ways over time and culture. The primary premise in support of this thesis is that, as one strategy of domination, dominating groups employ and perpetuate imperial myths that configure and establish social order and cultural hierarchy in their favor (insider/outsider, powerful/powerless, clean/unclean, chosen people, Manifest Destiny, and so on). The second, reciprocal premise is that dominated peoples respond to this ordering by adopting and subverting the very myths used to dominate them. This is especially true of the Bible and biblical interpretation.[4]

A conflation of these premises, then, contends that imperial myths can be used both to justify and deconstruct claims to power. On this matter, Robert Schreiter notes that

> forms are often borrowed from the ruling class, but are given
> different meanings and roles within the subaltern system. . . .
> The subaltern approach highlights an important aspect of
> popular religion often overlooked, namely, that the symbolic
> world of a popular religion can provide one of the few
> resources of identity over which an oppressed people can
> exercise some control over their own.[5]

A close examination of this wielding of and response to power will highlight what James Scott has so eloquently called "domination and the arts of resistance."[6] What is most fascinating about his examination of negotiations of power is that these claims to power are exactly what serve as the impetus for counterdiscourses. On this didactic relationship, Vincent Wimbush notes that

> if power is really power insofar as it is comprehensive, sedimented, or profoundly, deeply embedded within every aspect of social order, with the purpose of holding all constitutive elements in place, then there must first always be resistance to it.[7]

Wimbush also proposes that the general dynamics of the power play and reaction to it are fairly stable over time. The phenomenon is cross-cultural and cross-temporal. This observation is especially valuable with respect to the following chapters, which compare three historical moments separated by over nineteen centuries.[8]

I test my thesis over three distinct historical periods and geographical locations, surveying specific literary and artistic productions: (1) first-century Asia Minor, reading Revelation 12 against the Greco-Roman Dragon Slayer myth;[9] (2) seventeenth-century Mexico City, reading Creole priest Miguel Sanchez's *Imagen de la Virgen Maria* (1648) against the Spanish Virgin of Guadalupe myth, and Creole priest Luis Laso de la Vega's *Huei tlamahuiçoltica* (1649) against both the Spanish Virgin of Guadalupe myth and Sanchez's *Imagen;* and (3) twentieth-century East Los Angeles, reading *El Plan Espiritual de Aztlán* (1969)[10] and Chicana/o public art against the U.S. mythology of Manifest Destiny. I have selected these three moments for study because there is a direct genealogical relationship amongst the three counterdiscourses of Revelation 12, Sanchez's *Imagen* and Laso de la Vega's *Huei tlamahuiçoltica*, and Chicana/o public art. That is, the later texts are direct rereadings and reappropriations of Revelation 12.

THE BEGINNING: REVELATION 12

The book of Revelation is deeply embedded in imperial ideology. A postcolonial approach to chapter 12 will demonstrate that, at least on one level, this chapter is a retelling, reconfiguration, and subversion of the Greco-Roman Dragon Slayer myth that was important to Roman imperial ideology in Asia Minor in the first century of the Common Era.[11] I further demonstrate that seventeenth-century Mexico and twentieth-century East Los Angeles exhibit similar patterns of power (re)negotiation.

The subsequent connection between Revelation 12 and its New World (Mexican and Chicana/o) counterparts is made explicitly by a Creole priest, Miguel Sánchez, who records in his *Imagen de la Virgen Maria* (1648) that the Mexican Virgin was a faithful copy of the image of Mary seen by John the Evangelist and described in chapter 12 of the book of Revelation.[12] This relationship is also established by the Spanish artist Francisco Pacheco, who in 1649 served as inspector of painting for the Inquisition at Seville. In a text entitled *El arte de la pintura: Su antigüedad y grandeza*, Pacheco specifically directed Spanish painters to employ the woman of Revelation 12 as their guide to painting the Virgin Mary as part of the Counter-Reformation.[13] Extrapolating from Sánchez in 1649, another Creole priest, Luis Laso de la Vega, composed his *Huei tlamahuiçoltica* to promote an indigenous agenda in New Spain. Laso de la Vega's literary depiction of Mary ultimately served as guide to subsequent Marian representations in New Spain and was transformed in Creole and indigenous sensibilities into the *Mexican* Virgin of Guadalupe.

This act of subversion with respect to both the Spanish and the emerging Creole class serves as the model for twentieth-century artistic depictions of the Virgin of Guadalupe in East Los Angeles. And as in first-century Asia Minor, these subsequent depictions of Mary are examples of the periphery signifying back at and in defiance of the imperialistic ideologies of the center. I therefore establish a cross-temporal and cross-cultural dialogue amongst all three moments in the hope that ancient history will illuminate modern history and, conversely, that modern history will illuminate ancient history.

POSTCOLONIAL BIBLICAL CRITICISM

One main purpose of this book is to challenge previously constructed histories that do not recognize the socially located and hermeneutic realities of the marginalized. My choice of interpretive methodology is of paramount importance for constructing this ideological challenge. Likewise, the situation also calls for the reader to be suspicious of any interpretive method developed during the apex of European colonialism—in short, any method that favors the dominant society. Enrique Dussel comments, "Modernity appears when Europe affirms itself as the 'center' of a World History that it inaugurates; the 'periphery' that surrounds this center is consequently part of its self-definition."[14]

What, if any, methodologies challenge those that emerged with the rise of modernity or appeared during the decline of European colonialism—counterdiscourses that might be relevant for a study such as this? A survey of the interpretive landscape of contemporary biblical studies suggests that postcolonial biblical criticism is most suited to the task. According to R. S. Sugirtharajah,

> the greatest single aim of postcolonial biblical criticism is to situate colonialism at the centre of the Bible and biblical interpretation. What we find in both the historical and the hermeneutical literature of biblical scholarship over the last four hundred years is the impact of the Reformation or the Counter-reformation, or the effects of the Enlightenment in defining and shaping the discipline by rationalistic thinking or its offshoot, historical criticism. But there has been a remarkable unwillingness to mention imperialism as shaping the contours of biblical scholarship. What postcolonial biblical criticism does is to focus on the whole issue of expansion, domination, and imperialism as central forces in defining both biblical narratives and biblical interpretation.[15]

He continues by noting that the specific usefulness of postcolonial biblical criticism "lies in its capacity to detect oppression, expose misrepresentation, and to promote a fairer world rather than in its sophistry, precision, and its erudite qualities as a critical tool."[16]

My use of postcolonial biblical criticism, therefore, involves a twofold agenda. First, postcolonial biblical criticism is the most capable of bringing to light the colonial entanglements of the Bible and biblical interpretation, thereby facilitating the examination of power relations in the three historical periods proposed. Second, postcolonial biblical criticism, as a criticism in contrast to a theory, can be framed as "life-enhancing and constitutively opposed to every form of tyranny, domination, and abuse," with "social goals [that] are noncoercive knowledge produced in the interest of human freedom."[17] As a result, my further intention is to lay the groundwork for opposition that will explicitly challenge ideologies that are oppressive and harmful to people. The value of this methodological approach is its practical nature—the movement away from a strictly theoretical approach to a praxis-centered, liberative form of sociocultural criticism.

To apply Sugirtharajah's theoretical positions on postcolonial biblical criticism, I have juxtaposed them with the following key postcolonial concepts: hybridity, mimicry, and ambivalence. Employment of these terms will make Sugirtharajah's ideological ruminations more tangible. The following quotation is a succinct summation of the concept of hybridity:

> One of the most widely employed and most disputed terms in post-colonial theory, hybridity commonly refers to the creation of new transcultural forms within the contact zone produced by colonization. As used in horticulture, the term refers to the cross-breeding of two species by grafting or cross-pollination to form a third, "hybrid" species. Hybridization takes many forms: linguistic, cultural, political, racial, etc.[18]

The concept of mimicry is summarized as follows:

> *Mimicry* is an increasingly important term in post-colonial theory, because it has come to describe the ambivalent relationship between colonizer and colonized. When colonial discourse encourages the colonized subject to "mimic" the colonizer, by adopting the colonizer's cultural habits, assumptions, institutions and values, the result is never simple reproduction of those traits. Rather, the result is a "blurred copy" of the colonizer that can be quite threatening. This is because mimicry is never far from mockery, since it can appear to parody [distort, ridicule, satirize] whatever it mimics. Mimicry therefore locates a crack in the certainty of colonial dominance, an uncertainty in its control of the behaviour of the colonized.[19]

Perhaps the most important and relevant concept for this book is ambivalence:

> [Ambivalence] describes the complex mix of attraction and repulsion that characterizes the relationship between colonizer and colonized. The relationship is ambivalent because the colonized subject is never simply and completely opposed to the colonizer. Rather than assuming that some colonized subjects are "complicit" and some "resistant," ambivalence suggests that complicity and resistance exists in a fluctuating relation with the colonial subject.[20]

These concepts force us to think more accurately about the simple dualities of "center" and "margin/periphery," and they make us a party to the actual multi-texturedness of cultural contacts. This multi-texturedness provides insight into those in-between spaces where power is generally brokered and negotiated, a window into those "transcultural forms within the contact zone"[21] where both benign and acute forms of mimicry play out.

In addition to adopting a postcolonial biblical approach, I also draw on the work of political scientist James Scott, who teases out the hidden dimensions of power-laden colonial encounters. He argues that

> every subordinate group creates out of its ordeal, a "hidden transcript" that represents a critique of power spoken behind the back of the dominant . . . it is a discourse that cannot be spoken in the face of power. . . . [However,] "public transcript" is a shorthand way of describing the open interaction between subordinates and those who dominate. The public transcript, where it is not positively misleading, is unlikely to tell the whole story about power relations. It is frequently in the interest of both parties to tacitly conspire in misrepresentations . . . the more menacing the power, the thicker the mask.[22]

Scott's work is challenging in that it forces the critic away from overliteral interpretations of texts and textual performances. Therefore, to analyze how a peripheral group negotiates and critiques the power of the dominant, the critic must, when possible, go "backstage," where subversive discourse can be safely promoted. Any analysis of public discourse without the nuance encouraged by Scott might then take diversion and misrepresentation as an actual reaction to power. Because of the unequal power dynamic between center and periphery, Scott proposes that explicit defiance on the part of the periphery is extremely rare. He therefore suggests that we look to other avenues to see demonstrations of how the periphery acts defiantly:

> Most forms of this struggle stop well short of outright collective defiance. Here I have in mind the ordinary weapons of relatively powerless groups: foot-dragging, dissimulation, desertion, false compliance [subversion], pilfering, feigned ignorance, slander, arson, sabotage, and so on.[23]

Scott's work challenges the reader to use caution when evaluating the performance that I am calling the "subversion of imperial myths."[24] Do we categorize these subversions as public or private performances? The relevance of this categorization is that it then determines the degree of literalness we can employ in approaching these texts. If the subversive performance is meant for general public consumption, a greater degree of caution is necessary (as in the case with the murals of East Los Angeles). If these are indeed private performances, we would expect a greater degree of an unveiled critique of power. However, we must also consider that since we will also be analyzing literary productions, what may have been written as private transcript would incorporate a dimension of illusion and code. In other words, offstage spoken discourse can be much more explicit in its critique of power because it has not been committed to writing and theoretically leaves no trace of existence. Writing, in contrast, is not afforded the luxury of this sublimity but, instead, intends a level of permanence by its very transcription.

Finally, I seek also to challenge the manner in which postcolonial discourse has been framed. Historically, postcolonial criticism has focused on European encounters whose genesis was eighteenth- and nineteenth-century exploration—namely, those incited by non-Iberian colonizers (England, Denmark, France, and so on). This exclusion has disregarded the role that Spain and Portugal played in modeling colonial aspirations. As a result, postcolonial conversations concerning Latin America have been at best limited in the arena of modern postcolonial critique. Enrique Dussel contends thus:

> I have said that the concept of modernity occludes the role of Europe's own Iberian periphery, and in particular Spain, in its formation. At the end of the fifteenth century, Spain was the only European power with the capacity of external territorial conquest. . . . Understanding this, I believe, allows Latin America to also rediscover its "place" in the history of modernity. We were the first periphery of modern Europe; that is, we suffered globally from our moment of origin on a constitutive process of modernization.[25]

The recognition that European modernity begins not in the eighteenth or nineteenth century but in 1492 invites excluded continents—the Americas—into formal discourse and critique with our Asian, African, and European counterparts.

PLAN OF THE BOOK

The focus of chapter 1 is to establish the Greco-Roman Dragon Slayer myth as prior to and one impetus for the Christian composition of Revelation 12. Therefore, the establishment of this myth is the first order of business of chapter 1. Once the contents of the myth are established, I will argue for the Roman privileging of the Dragon Slayer myth in early imperial propaganda. I then attempt to delineate the *Sitz im Leben* (situation in life) that gave rise to a Christian appropriation and subversion of the Dragon Slayer myth in the first century of the Common Era. Finally, chapter 1 will demonstrate that the twelfth chapter of the book of Revelation was written in part as a direct response to the imperial employment of the Dragon Slayer myth.

Chapter 2 begins by establishing Revelation 12 as the literary model for subsequent artistic representations of the Virgin of Guadalupe in New Spain. It also focuses on the Spanish devotion to the Virgin of Guadalupe prior to the Spaniards, coming to New Spain, thereby establishing that Guadalupan devotion in Spain preceded any such worship in the Americas.

Once this fact is established, it is then possible to construct how and why Creoles of the New World found the Virgin of Guadalupe's subversion to be of value to them. This discussion focuses on the Americanized accounts of the apparition, *Imagen de la Virgen Maria*, written by Miguel Sánchez in 1648, and the *Huei tlamahuiçoltica*, the almost immediate response to it, written by Luis Laso de la Vega in 1649.

Chapter 3 begins the analysis of the final site of resistance for this project: East Los Angeles in the 1960s and '70s. This chapter takes an in-depth look at the production of the document *El Plan Espiritual de Aztlán* as a countermythology to the U.S. notion of "Manifest Destiny." It also assesses the employment of the iconography of the Virgin of Guadalupe in public art as a symbol of resistance. These murals, although polyvalent in meaning today, were initially representative of shrouded acts of resistance in the face of oppression. I therefore attempt to excavate the earliest meaning(s) of Guadalupe's artistic representations in East Los Angeles. I then relate these public art forms to the epoch of Mexican muralism of the early twentieth century in order to establish this genre of art as highly political and defiant.

The final chapter summarizes and compares the three historical moments discussed in the previous chapters through the lens of postcolonial biblical criticism, thereby highlighting the colonial entanglements of biblical texts and their interpretations. It primarily establishes seventeenth-century Mexico and twentieth-century East Los Angeles as moments of subversion in their responses to colonial or neocolonial power. Finally, I discuss this overall project as a moment of liberation in the ever-present reality of contemporary Empire.

CHAPTER 1

SUBVERTING AN IMPERIAL MYTH IN FIRST-CENTURY ASIA MINOR: THE DRAGON SLAYER

THE PRE-ROMAN MYTH IN ASIA MINOR

THE IMPERIAL MYTHS OF ANTIQUITY and today evoke countermythologies established by the marginalized. With this chapter, I begin in antiquity by considering the Dragon Slayer myth as foundational for the construction of a new Roman imperial identity. This Greek myth was used at the apex of Roman attempts to reorder the post-republic era after the assassination of Julius Caesar in 44 B.C.E. and the rise of Augustus Caesar subsequent to his defeat of Marc Antony in the battle of Actium in 31 B.C.E. Rome appropriated the earlier Dragon Slayer myth to claim a genealogical relationship between the new emperor and the god Apollo. According to the histories and archaeology of the early principate, Apollo, the prototypical emperor, would establish the Golden Age of Rome. All subsequent emperors would justify their reigns by that model.

Subjects of the empire were well aware of the power of this mythical motif and understood that effective diatribes against emperor and empire could begin only with a critique of this foundational myth. This was certainly the case on at least two occasions, for the Jewish and Christian scribes in the early empire brilliantly yet covertly subverted this Roman version of the Dragon Slayer myth in a Jewish apocalypse and, subsequently, the Christian Revelation to John. The Jewish author replaces the role of Apollo by inserting the Jewish Messiah as the protagonist. The

Christian author raises the ante by suggesting that Jesus Christ specifically assumes the role of the messianic protagonist. He amplifies his argument by incorporating the heavenly imagery of another Greco-Roman myth, the Dragon Subjugator myth[1], so as to move the conflict from the realm of the earthly and political to a heightened cosmic struggle between the Lamb of God and Satan.

The form of the Dragon Slayer myth employed by most contemporary scholars is based on a work attributed to Gaius Julius Hyginus (first century B.C.E.), namely, his *Fabulae* 140 (*Fabularum Liber*)[2]:

> Python: Python, offspring of Terra, was a huge dragon who, before the time of Apollo, used to give oracular responses in Mt. Parnassus. Death was fated to come to him from the offspring of Latona. At that time, Jove lay with Latona [Gk: Leto], daughter of Polus. When Juno found this out, she decreed [?] (*facit*) that Latona should give birth at a place where the sun did not shine. When Python knew that Latona was pregnant by Jove, he followed her to kill her. But by the order of Jove the wind Aquilo carried her away, and bore her to Neptune. He protected her, but in order not to make void Juno's decree, he took her to the island Ortygia and covered the islands with waves. When Python did not find her, he returned to Parnassus. But Neptune brought the island of Ortygia up to a higher position; it was later called the island of Delos. There Latona, clinging to an olive tree, bore Apollo and Diana, to whom Vulcan gave arrows as gifts. Four days after they were born, Apollo exacted vengeance for his mother. He went to Parnassus and slew Python with arrows. (Because of this deed he is called Pythian.) He put Python's bones in a caldron, deposited them in his temple and instituted funeral games for him which are called Pythian.[3]

Most commentators have noted some degree of similarity between Revelation 12 and this form of the Dragon Slayer myth. In this chapter, I contend that both the Dragon Slayer myth and the Dragon Subjugator myth are intricately embedded in the final redaction of Revelation 12, rather than that one of these myths dominates Revelation 12 to the exclusion of the other. I also propose that Revelation 12 in its final form is the product of at least two redactional moments, one Jewish and one Christian.

Establishing the content of the Dragon Slayer myth is necessary to reconstruct both the Jewish and also the later Christian subversive redaction of this text. We must therefore ask why Hyginus's form of the myth has become popular among modern commentators. Various forms of this myth circulated in antiquity, including Hesiod's *The Homeric Hymns* to Apollo (Delian III and Pythian Apollo IV, 8th–7th centuries B.C.E.)[4] and the myths of Theogonis lines 1-10 (6th century B.C.E.),[5] Pindar's Pythian Odes IV and VII (6th–5th centuries B.C.E.),[6] Herodotus' *Herodotus* II lines 156-7 (5th century B.C.E.),[7] Euripides' *Iphengenia in Taurus* 1234 ff. (5th century B.C.E.),[8] Callimachus' *Hymn to Apollo and Hymn to Delos* (3rd century B.C.E.),[9] Apollodorus I, IV, 1 (1st century B.C.E./C.E.),[10] Plutarch's *Moralia* (1st century C.E.),[11] Pausanias II, 7, 7 and II, 30, 3 (2nd century C.E.),[12] and Lucian's *Dialogues of the Sea Gods* 9 (10) (2nd century C.E.).[13] However, not all of these forms of the myth contain the various elements that came to be embedded in Revelation 12.

Relevant here are allusions to the birth of Apollo in conjunction with the rivalry with the dragon, especially in later versions of the myth. The Homeric Hymn to Pythian Apollo mentions the birth but not the dragon. The hymn to Delian Apollo begins with a grown Apollo, making no mention of his birth, but there is a slaying of a female dragon. Theogonis makes no mention of the dragon but does mention the birth. Pindar also omits any mention of the dragon in his hymn. In the work of Herodotus, there is no mention of the birth, Leto is not the mother of Apollo (although she does protect him from Typhon), and Apollo is the son of Osiris. In Euripides' account, we see the early yet incomplete merging of the birth and dragon narratives. In this account, the baby Apollo slays the dragon, but the motivation is not revenge. The dragon never pursues Leto; rather, the execution of the dragon is accomplished so that Apollo might take over the oracle. Callimachus, like the Homeric Hymns, separates the two motifs. In his hymn to Apollo, there is a vague reference to the birth of

Apollo in conjunction with the slaying of the dragon. In his hymn to Delos, he explicitly mentions the birth of Apollo, but with no mention of the dragon. In Apollodorus's account, the two motifs appear together, but there is no interaction between the two. Plutarch makes no explicit mention of the birth but deals extensively with the slaying of the dragon.

In the first century C.E., the fusion of the birth and dragon motifs was explicitly made as attested by Lucian: "There [Parnassus] Apollo, with yet unpracticed shafts, laid low the Python and so avenged his mother, who had been driven forth when great with child."[14]

The accounts of Pausanius and Lucian also postdate Revelation 12 but are still valuable for this study on the issue of the relation between the motifs of the birth and the dragon. Pausanius recognizes the struggle between Apollo and Python but says nothing of the birth of Apollo. Finally, Lucian makes explicit reference, as does Hyginus, to the relationship linking the pursuit of Leto, the birth of Apollo, and the slaying of the dragon.[15]

The two motifs, birth and dragon, are fused primarily in the later versions of the myth, producing a pattern that suggests the fusion is a later phenomenon than Revelation 12. This calls into question the nature of the interaction between Revelation 12 and the Dragon Slayer myth. If this fusion of motifs is indeed a later phenomenon, what evidence survives that a conflation of these two motifs existed in the first century of the Common Era? To solve this problem, it is necessary to consider nonliterary evidence for the fusion of these two motifs prior to Lucian and Hyginus.

	Birth of Apollo	Rivalry with the Dragon	Conflation of Themes
Homeric Hymn to Pythian Apollo (8th–7th centuries B.C.E.)	✓		
Homeric Hymn to Delian Apollo (8th–7th centuries B.C.E.)		✓	
Theogonis (6th century B.C.E.)	✓		
Pindar (6th–5th centuries B.C.E.)	✓		
Herodotus (5th century B.C.E.)		✓	
Euripides (5th century B.C.E.)	✓	✓	
Callimachus: Apollo (3rd century B.C.E.)	✓ (vague)	✓	✓ (vague)
Callimachus: Delos (3rd century B.C.E.)	✓		
Apollodorus (1st century B.C.E./C.E.)	✓	✓	
Plutarch (1st century C.E.)		✓	
Pausanius (2nd century C.E.)		✓	
Lucian (2nd century C.E.)	✓	✓	✓
Hyginus (2nd century C.E.)	✓	✓	✓
Lucian (1st century C.E.)	✓	✓	✓

Table 1   Birth of Apollo and rivalry with the dragon: relationship between the motifs in antiquity

One source of nonliterary evidence is found on two vases from the sixth or fifth century B.C.E. that, as described by Theodor Schreiber in *Apollon Pythoktonos*, depict the infant Apollo in the arms of Leto in juxtaposition with the dragon.[16] In one of these vase paintings, Apollo is depicted with his bow. This early evidence that the motifs of birth and dragon were seen in conjunction with each other suggests the possibility that the Jewish and Christian redactors were aware of a fusion of these two motifs. Indeed, W. K. Hedrick asserts, "These two vase paintings show that the separate myths were merged as early as the sixth or fifth century B.C."[17]

Schreiber describes a second account of nonliterary evidence for a merger of these two motifs, a group of twelve coins from antiquity.[18] On all of these coins, Leto is depicted fleeing while holding her two children. On four of the coins, Apollo is carrying his bow and arrows. Hedrick argues that the nonpictured pursuer in these coins must be Python since, according to the myth, it could be only Hera or Python. Yet, all four of these coins are dated toward the middle of the third century, and W. K. Hedrick notes that they are all from Asia Minor. Hedrick concludes, "The non-literary evidence collected by Schreiber argues for the existence of the myth, in a form something like that described in Lucian and Hyginus, in Asia Minor toward the end of the first century A.D."[19]

Although the evidence is limited, I argue that the Jewish and Christian appropriation of the Dragon Slayer myth was indeed a borrowing of an earlier myth and not the original work of either redactor. This contention will be established by pointing out the value of the Dragon Slayer myth for imperial propaganda and the value of subverting such a myth to those on the margins of the Roman Empire. This argument is solidified by Adela Yarbro Collins's proposal that the Dragon Slayer myth was firmly established in Western Asia Minor before the conclusion of the first century C.E.[20]

It is thus apparent from literary and nonliterary evidence that the Dragon Slayer myth as preserved in Hyginus's *Fabulae* with its juxtaposition of the birth of Apollo and the slaying of the dragon was the form of the myth used in the redactional work of the Jewish and Christian appropriators. (The Jewish and Christian texts that I will discuss in this chapter contain both the birth and dragon motifs.) But before I consider these redactions, let us survey the use of the Dragon Slayer myth in imperial propaganda—that is, the myth that will be subverted.

THE MYTH IN ROMAN IMPERIAL PROPAGANDA

With the assassination of Julius Caesar in 44 B.C.E., the Roman Republic fell into a period of destructive civil war. This period was accompanied by a shift in religiopolitical propaganda. Octavian, the adopted son of Julius, records in his autobiography that in July 44 B.C.E., a star appeared in the heavens for a period of seven days. In retrospect, this occasion was seen as evidence for the apotheosis of Julius. Octavian, with the blessing of the Roman senate, obtained permission to enter his father into the state cult, and from that moment, he would claim the title *divi filius* (son of god). This was a remarkable claim during civil war, when the succession to power in the Roman Republic could now be pursued by the son of the assassinated god. This claim, however, was not uncontested. Marc Antony, who was popular in the eastern provinces, after his victorious battles in Armenia claimed the title *neos Dionysus* (young, new Dionysus).[21] Thus, began the rivalry between the two competing factions for the rule of Rome, a rivalry that would last until the battle of Actium in 31 B.C.E.

During this time, the myth(s) of Apollo become embedded in imperial ideology. Miraculous claims were made about Octavian as a youth. [22] During the power vacuum, Octavian and Marc Antony were involved not only in military campaigns against each other but also in propaganda campaigns to buttress their aspirations to ascend to the highest level of Roman power.[23] Octavian added to these claims by taking on the role of protégé of Apollo. Paul Zanker notes, "This process was taken further in Octavian's struggle with his opponent, Antony, the alter ego of Dionysus, and eventually developed into the mythological foundation of his later role of Augustus."[24] Imperial propaganda had begun.

After the defeat of Antony at the battle of Actium in 31 B.C.E., this mythological framework became even more developed. Proponents of Octavian, now Augustus, incorporated the seal of the sphinx, a symbol of the *regnum Apollonis* (reign, kingdom of Apollo) in Augustan art.[25] After 30 B.C.E., tales circulated about the miraculous birth of Augustus. Zanker recounts, "Octavian's mother Atia had conceived the boy not by his putative father, but by the god [Apollo] in the form of the snake. The same had been said of Olympias, mother of Alexander the Great."[26] Augustus also attributes his victory over Pompey to Apollo and his sister Diana (Artemis). Again Zanker notes, "It is fascinating to observe how deliberately Octavian pursued this relationship to Apollo over the next twenty years or . . . how his sense of mission for healing Rome's wounds bore the stamp of Apollo."[27] The connection between Augustus and Apollo became explicitly clear when Augustus built the Temple of Apollo immediately adjacent to his own residence. Recent archaeological evidence suggests that a connecting ramp existed between the two structures.[28] Many of the goals and objectives of the reign of Augustus bear the stamp of Apollo. The bringer of the *pax Romana* and the new Golden Age of Rome is reminiscent of Apollo, the deity who was to usher in the Golden Age.

There is evidence that Nero also adapted this Apollonian mythological framework. Hedrick makes the following observations regarding Nero presenting himself as Apollo:

> Tacitus has disparaging remarks about Nero's playing the lyre under the appearance of Apollo [Tacitus, *Annals* 14.14]. Suetonius tells of Nero's returning from Greece with the Pythian crown and having statues and coins produced with himself as lyre-player. This seems to be something more than a musician's vanity; the procession went straight to the temple of Apollo for celebration [Suetonius, *Nero* 25]. Cassius Dio tells us of the cries that greeted Nero on two separate arrivals. In the first one there were, he reports, hired cheerleaders. "Glorious Caesar! Our Apollo, our Augustus, another Pythian . . ." [Cassius Dio 62.29.5]. "Hail Olympian Victor! Augustus! Augustus! Hail to Nero our Hercules! Hail to Nero our Apollo!" [Cassius Dio, 63.20.5].[29]

In addition, the British Museum has a coin from Sardis with the images of Nero and Apollo on opposite sides.[30] The adoption of Apollonian imagery during the reign of Nero is well documented. Yarbro Collins even asserts, "Nero associated his own person with Apollo much more blatantly than Augustus had done."[31] The incorporation of Apollonian mythology is well documented for the reigns of Augustus and Nero, as well as those of several other emperors.

What was the intrinsic value of this myth for imperial ideology and propaganda? On this matter, Eugene Boring is quite explicit:

> The Roman emperors found the myth politically useful. Apollo was understood as the primeval king who reigned over the "golden age" of peace and prosperity. Augustus, the first emperor, interpreted his own rule in terms of this tradition, claiming that his administration was the Golden Age and casting himself as the new Apollo. [Likewise,] Nero erected statues to himself as the new Apollo. There were coins in which the radiance of the sun god emanates from [Nero's] head. A grateful citizen of the Roman world could readily think of the story as a reflection of his or her own experience, with the following cast: the woman [in the story] is the goddess Roma, the queen of heaven; the son is the emperor, who kills the dragon and founds the new golden age; the dragon represents the power of darkness.[32]

The appropriation of the Dragon Slayer myth by Augustus and Nero allows the reader/hearer to think of the emperor when Apollo is narrated as the primary protagonist in the myth. Leto's function is basically limited to the passive role of being pursued by Python and being assisted by Zeus before actively giving birth to Apollo. Her main function in the myth is maternal. By contrast, Python functions as the primary adversary of the woman and the child and, therefore, emerges as the story's principal antagonistic actor. It is, therefore, Apollo's role to actively subjugate and defeat Python as the myth's primary hero.

Is it then possible that the specific allusion to the Dragon Slayer myth in Augustan propaganda can be related to his subduing of his rival Marc Antony at Actium in 31 B.C.E.? Or perhaps it was related to Octavian's bringing of order (the dragon explicitly references chaos) after the civil wars within the new empire or his subduing of piracy and/or banditry within Roman territories. I suggest that the Dragon Slayer myth is adaptable enough to fit any situation or crisis that Augustus—or any other subsequent emperor—might desire to resolve. Therefore, the Dragon Slayer myth sets the ideological framework for the demonization of the enemy, providing the necessary sentiment and logic to destroy it. As a result, the "dragon" can be any imperial antagonist; the Dragon Slayer Myth was highly adaptable. Whoever or whatever is viewed as antagonistic or threatening toward the empire could and would be labeled, at least ideologically, as representative of the dragon, as anti-imperial, and as chaos.

This was a new era in Roman sensibilities. It was a time when the Roman civil wars were a thing of the past and when subsequent emperors benefited from the peace and prosperity of this new age. The Dragon Slayer myth with its protagonist Apollo, the vanguard of the expected new era, and its chaotic rival, the dragon, was well suited to convey this new sense of Roman destiny.

JEWISH SUBVERSION OF THE DRAGON SLAYER MYTH

My point of departure for the Jewish and the Christian subversions of the Dragon Slayer myth is Revelation 12, a text paradigmatic of (re) negotiation of power:

> [1] And a great portent appeared in heaven, a woman clothed with the sun, with the moon under her feet, and on her head a crown of twelve stars. [2]She was pregnant and was crying out in birth pangs, in the agony of giving birth. [3]Then another portent appeared in heaven: a great red dragon, with seven heads and ten horns, and seven diadems on his heads. [4]His tail swept down a third of the stars of heaven and threw them to the earth. Then the dragon stood before the woman who was about to bear a child, so that he might devour her child as soon as it was born. [5]And she gave birth to a son, who is to rule all the nations with a rod of iron. But her child was snatched away and taken to God and to his throne; [6]and the woman fled into the wilderness, where she has a place prepared by God, so that there she can be nourished for one thousand two hundred and sixty days.
>
> [7] Now war broke out in heaven, Michael and his angels fought against the dragon. The dragon and his angels fought back, [8]but they were defeated and there was no longer any

place for them in heaven. [9]The great dragon was thrown down, that ancient serpent, who is called the Devil and Satan, the deceiver of the whole world—he was thrown down to the earth, and his angels were thrown down with him.

[10]Then I heard a loud voice in heaven, proclaiming, "Now have come the salvation and the power and the kingdom of our God and the authority of his Messiah, for the accuser of our comrades has been thrown down, who accuses them day and night before our God. [11]But they have conquered him by the blood of the Lamb and by the word of their testimony, for they did not cling to life even in the face of death. [12]Rejoice then, you heavens and those that dwell in them! But woe to the earth and the sea, for the devil has come down to you with great wrath, because he knows that his time is short!"

[13]So when the dragon saw that he had been thrown down to the earth, he pursued the woman who had given birth to the male child. [14]But the woman was given the two wings of the great eagle, so that she could fly from the serpent into the wilderness, to her place where she is nourished for a time, and times, and half a time. [15]Then from his mouth the serpent poured water like a river after the woman, to sweep her away with the flood. [16]But the earth came to the help of the woman; it opened its mouth and swallowed the river that the dragon had poured from his mouth. [17]Then the dragon was angry with the woman, and went off to make war on the rest of her children, those who keep the commandments of God and hold the testimony to Jesus. [18]And he stood on the sand of the sea.[33]

The redaction history of Revelation 12 has long been a contentious issue. The first commentator to propose that the body of Revelation 12 was taken from an earlier Jewish source was Eberhard Vischer in 1886.[34] Working independently of Vischer, G. J. Weyland also concluded that Revelation 12 was originally Jewish.[35] This presupposition was later supported by Friedrich Spitta, Johannes Weiss, Julius Wellhausen, and Adela Yarbro Collins.[36] Detractors of this hypothesis include Wilhelm Bousset and Ernst Lohmeyer.[37]

The redaction history of Revelation 12 is extremely important for assessing the likelihood of a Jewish subversion of imperial myths. On this issue, Yarbro Collins argues, "Revelation [12] can be and obviously has for many centuries been read from a Christian point of view. But the probabilities are *clearly against the theory that the chapter as a whole was originally composed by a Christian.*"[38] She begins her argument by stating that Revelation 12:5 is clearly a messianic allusion to Psalm 2:9, thus prompting her to speculate whether "the description of the messiah and his role in these verses conform well enough to the kerygma to make it probable that the passage was formulated by a Christian."[39] She concludes her assessment of the adaptation of the messiah motif with this assertion:

> The anomalies are serious enough to indicate that the passage was not originally formulated by a Christian. The story is concerned with the *birth*, not with the *death* of the messiah. The child is translated to God to rescue him from a threat at a time of his *birth*. Since the translation takes place immediately following the birth, it could not have been intended originally as a reference to the ascension of Christ (which is the usual—ancient and modern—Christian understanding of the passage). The absence of any reference to the life and deeds of the messiah, especially the lack of any notice of a redemptive death, and the complete projection of the messianic office of the child into the future, make it quite unlikely that the narrative concerning the woman, the dragon and the child was originally composed to suit a Christian context.[40]

The argument is further enhanced with an assessment of the role of the woman in her original context. Again, the woman's identity is obfuscated from a Christian perspective. How could she simultaneously be mother both of the Messiah and of the persecuted church? From a Jewish perspective, however, the woman can be interpreted singularly as the "persecuted people of God from whom comes the messiah."[41] Based on this analysis, Yarbro Collins convincingly concludes that at least a portion of Revelation 12, most notably verses 1–6 and 13–17, were originally adapted from a Jewish source.

A central contention of this thesis of a Jewish component in Revelation 12 is that there was messianic expectation among at least one faction of Jews in Asia Minor in the century before the production of Revelation.[42] Caution is called for, however. James Charlesworth notes that the term *Messiah* "is rarely found, and the functions or attributes of the 'Messiah' are even less explained in extant pre-70 Jewish documents."[43] Moreover, scholars today reject the earlier false assumption that Judaism was a monolithic entity with a unified "messianic" expectation.[44] Conversely, however, conclusions drawn by Richard Horsley that there was minimal or no interest in a messiah or a general messianic expectation in the late Second Temple period may also be overstated.[45]

I do not argue for a comprehensive Jewish expectation of a messiah or messianic figure in pre-70 Asia Minor, nor do I accept the minimalist position taken by Charlesworth and others. My compromise position is based on the work of such scholars as John J. Collins and James D. G. Dunn, who focus on pre-70 texts, namely, the Dead Sea Scrolls, *Psalms of Solomon*, *4 Ezra*, and *2 Baruch*.[46] For both scholars, the roots of a non-eschatological messianic expectation are well grounded in the Hebrew Bible (for example, 2 Sam. 7:12-13, 16; Isa. 11:1-2; Jer. 23:5, 33:15; Ezek. 34:24, 37:25). This expectation is still evident in postexilic times (Hag. 2:23; Zech. 3:8, 6:12). With the formal end of the Jerusalem monarchy, however, the expectation lay dormant during the period 500–200 B.C.E.[47]

According to Dunn, the revival of a royal messianic expectation occurs during the failed Hasmonean period. He cites *Pss. Sol.* 17:21-24 as the most striking example of this reemergence:

> See, Lord, and raise up for them their king, the son of David, to rule over your servant Israel in the time known to you, O God. Undergird him with the strength to destroy the unrighteous rulers, to purge Jerusalem from gentiles who trample her to destruction; in wisdom and in righteousness to drive out the sinners from the inheritance; to smash the arrogance of sinners like a potter's jar; to shatter their substance with an iron rod; to destroy the unlawful nations with the word of his mouth.[48]

Dunn goes on to note that the same messianic figure is later referred to in *Psalms of Solomon* as "their king . . . the Lord Messiah."[49] In the Dead Sea Scrolls, the promise of 2 Sam. 7:14 is well established in 4Q174 (4QFlor) 1:10-12. Messianic proclamations found in Isaiah, Jeremiah, and Ezekiel can be seen in 1QSb (1Q28b) 5:20; 1QM 5:1; 4Q161 (4QpIsa[a]) 3:18, 4Q174 (4QFlor) 1:11; 4Q252 5:3-4; CD 7:19-20; and 4Q285. Dunn also contends, "[What is] equally striking is Qumran's expectation of two messianic figures, the messiahs of Aaron and Israel, that is, a priestly Messiah and a royal Messiah, with the Messiah of Israel almost certainly to be identified as the royal Messiah."[50]

John Collins notes that the reinvigorated messianic expectation is also pronounced in *4 Ezra* (especially 7:28-29 and 13:1ff.) and *2 Baruch* (especially 2:34-35, 4:36-37, and 5:5ff.), both of which are independent of the Dead Sea Scrolls. Moreover, Josephus, in *War* 6.312, notes that the revolt of 62 C.E. was ignited by an ambiguous oracle in scripture. It is also important to note that "two royal pretenders . . . with a messianic aura in the Robber War [4/3 B.C.E.] throw the whole country into an uproar, . . . events [that] show better than any literary texts that messianic expectations were alive among the people."[51] Recall also that the military leader bar Kochba was given the title "messiah" in the Jewish Revolt of 132–35 C.E. Perhaps even more significant is Collins's observation of the transformation of messianic expectations that occurs in the book of Daniel:

> In Daniel [there] is a transformation in royal mythology. There is no role here for a Davidic king, and little for any human deliverer. The Maccabees are, at most, "a little help" (Dan. 11:34). There is a deliverer under God, but he operates on the heavenly level: the fate of Israel is determined by the battle between Michael and the princes of Greece and Persia (Dan. 10:20-21). This kind of transcendent, heavenly deliverer plays an increasingly important role in Jewish eschatology in the following centuries. It also provides a paradigm for messianic expectation that is quite different from the Davidic paradigm, although the two are *sometimes combined.*[52]

Based on these observations, Dunn asserts, "[The] conclusion looks to be well founded that in various strands of Judaism before and after Jesus there was a lively hope for the restoration of the Davidic line and that the Davidic Messiah was widely thought of as a warrior king who would destroy the enemies of Israel."[53]

Collins concludes, "The expectation of a Davidic messiah had a clear basis in the Scriptures, and became very widespread in various sectors of Judaism in the last century before the Common Era, in reaction to the rule of the Hasmoneans."[54] I prefer to speak more cautiously of the evidence enhancing the possibility of widespread messianic expectation at the time. Gerd Theissen and Annette Merz similarly conclude, "There was no such thing as Judaism and its messianic expectation in the singular; there were many Judaisms with different eschatological and messianic expectations."[55]

THE SITUATION OF THE JEWS IN ASIA MINOR

For a Jewish author to have felt compelled to appropriate and subvert a myth so central to imperial constructions of identity with "messianic" overtones was not without precedents. Yarbro Collins observes that

> Jesus ben Sirach made use of language apparently borrowed from an aretology of Isis in composing a hymn to wisdom (Sir 24:3-6). An Egyptian Jew, writing about the middle of the second century B.C.E., expressed his messianic hopes in language derived from Egyptian mythology: "And then from the sun God shall send a king . . ." (*Sib Or* 3:652). It is likely that another Jewish oracle in the third Sybil (3:350-80) contains language influenced by Isis aretologies.[56]

There are two different interpretations of the situation of the ancient Jewish diaspora in Asia Minor. The first, a conflict model, finds a comprehensive, sectarian Jewish separation from most facets of Greco-Roman society. Representative of this position is Victor Tcherikover:

> Scattered and dispersed among the nations, the Jews could maintain their existence and national features only as long as the organization of their internal life was of sufficient strength to *serve as a barrier* against the influence of the alien environment. . . . Thus in every land of the West where Jews

lived, organized Jewish communities were founded, and a form of public life was created which gave the people of Israel the strength to resist assimilation and which has survived— naturally with great changes—down to our day.[57]

Assessing this model, Philip A. Harland notes that

> some scholars interested in synagogues of the diaspora have viewed these groups as isolated and introverted communities living in a hostile environment. In this view, Jewish groups were sects in the sense that they were in a *consistent state of tension* with the surrounding society. . . . [They] emphasize the exclusivity of synagogues that ensured their protection from the syncretistic influences of an alien, Greco Roman environment.[58]

This conflict model, proposed by many scholars, is based primarily on the writings of several classical authors.[59] Examples of conflict between diaspora Jews and their Gentile neighbors are evident in Philostratus, *Life of Apollonius* 5.33; Justinus, *Epitoma Historiarum Philippcarum* 36.2.15; Quintillian, *Institutio Oratoria* 3.7.21; Petronius, *Satires* 68; and Tacitus, *History* 5.5. In the twentieth century, this model was the standard reconstruction of Jewish diaspora communities in antiquity, with its emphasis on the Jewish "tensions with and separation from" the Greco-Roman society in which it existed.

A major critic of this model is Philip A. Harland, who claims the following:

> This particular depiction of Christianity and diaspora Judaism as a largely uniform set of exclusive and sectarian groups serves to obscure rather than explain other evidence that suggests more complicated scenarios regarding the relationship between particular groups and the surrounding society. . . . The difficulties with these sectarian focused approaches to the social history of early Christianity and Judaism . . . is that they do not adequately account for primary [epigraphic and archaeological] evidence indicative of more complex possibilities in group-society interactions.[60]

The major contribution of Harland's work is his exhaustive attention to the epigraphic and archaeological evidence relevant to Jewish diaspora communities, especially in Asia Minor. What emerges from his work and that of like-minded scholars is a reimagining of the situation of diaspora Jews in antiquity.[61] Rather than positing a comprehensive scenario of conflict, Harland and others argue for a more accommodating and engaged diaspora Judaism, suggesting that "mounting evidence makes a sectarian reading of many synagogues and assemblies implausible."[62] In its place, they argue, "The emergent picture shows a variety of Jewish groups, many of which could be at home as participants in the polis despite their distinctive self-understandings and identities."[63] Paul Trebilco adds, "The Hellenistic polis accommodated considerable diversity of population without demanding uniformity . . . a degree of integration did not mean the abandonment of an active attention to Jewish tradition or distinctiveness."[64] Noteworthy here is that this new model, with its focus on Jewish accommodation, is still cognizant of the potential for problems between Jews and the state. References to "occasional civil disturbances" are not ruled out, and Trebilco goes on to recognize that "Jews who were significantly involved in city life must have encountered the problem posed for Jews by the all-pervasive presence of pagan cults in the city."[65] Harland, in agreement with Trebilco's assessment, adds, "Such evidence of positive relations does not preclude incidents when Jewish groups' relations with civic inhabitants or institutions or even Roman officials was rocky, especially in those unstable closing years of the late republic."[66]

Both Trebilco and Harland reject the conflict model while simultaneously arguing that sporadic tensions and/or hostilities were within the realm of possibility between Jews and their Gentile neighbors. This may be the strength of their position. They argue, based on epigraphic, literary, and archaeological evidence, for a more accommodating form of diaspora Judaism while recognizing that accommodation is not synonymous with submissiveness. Harland argues that hostilities between Jews and Romans may have been most acute during the period of the late republic, a period in which the Dragon Slayer myth functioned most acutely for Augustus's propaganda in his struggle against Antony.[67] We know also that the province of Asia Minor supported Antony in his power struggle with Octavian and was also hostile toward Rome during the failed invasion of Mithradates VI of Parthia in the first century B.C.E.

Another possible impetus for the writing of this specifically Jewish counter-myth was the sporadic poor relations between Jews and their Gentile neighbors. Rome reacted to Asia Minor's role in the Parthian invasion by implementing a severe tax by Sulla and plundering the regions suspected of supporting Parthia. This left the cities of Asia Minor in financial ruin. The devastation was so complete that the Asian population faced "such high rates of interest that they were forced to sell works of art, to mortgage public buildings and to suspend normal civic activities. Seventy years later there were buildings still lying in disrepair."[68] During this period, however, some Jews actually prospered financially, arousing jealousy on the part of their Gentile neighbors. John Barclay notes that

> at a time of financial stringency, with the cities only beginning to recover from decades of debt, it seems to have been extremely irksome to Greeks to witness this large and apparently wealthy community fail to pull their weight for the benefit of the city. The Jews made no contributions for the dilapidated temples in their own cities: they sent their money to a temple elsewhere. Indeed it appears that they refused in general to undertake certain "liturgy" obligations, which were normally required of wealthy citizens as their contribution to the welfare and honour of the city. In some cities the authorities took steps to rectify this "injustice"— with what legal proceedings we cannot now tell—and seized the temple collections in lieu of money they reckoned owing to them. The Jews bitterly resented such confiscations. . . . It appears that, so long as the financial crisis lasted, the Jews' large collections were too tempting a cherry to resist, and their apparent failure to assist in the economic restoration of their host cities continued to be a cause of resentment.[69]

This argument is supported by the "Speech of Nicolas" in Josephus's *Antiquities* 16.31-57. Nicolas protested in the presence of Agrippa that Greeks were confiscating the Temple tax that was to be sent to Jerusalem, a practice that had been going on for years in Asia Minor but became a major matter of contention with Asia's declining financial situation in the late first century B.C.E. Other issues that Nicolas specifically addresses are the preservation of the Jewish religious practices of sacrifice, festival, Sabbath observation, and judicial self-determination. Sabbath observation was invoked on various occasions for Jewish exemption from military service during the Roman civil wars. Also, from a Greek perspective, practices such as calendar, festival, and feast observances, which prevented Jews from participating in the rituals and routines of provincial life, became quite irksome to their non-Jewish neighbors. After the rise of the imperial period with its heightened expectations of imperial cult participation, the existence of such a large and prosperous community that stood apart from local practices was problematic and became a source of tension between the two groups. The tension was not so much based on Roman expectations but rather on how the provinces retained some powers for themselves and sought to establish imperial benefaction.[70]

In sum, the conflict model proposed by Tcherikover and others is less tenable than the model proposed by Harland and Trebilco. Although any marginalized group would attempt to accommodate local practices that they found least distasteful, this does not preclude the possibility of occasional upheavals in social order. Sociological studies, however, demonstrate that revolt is the exception rather than the rule. According to James Scott, the center and periphery simultaneously conspire in misrepresentations to accommodate each other's problematic coexistence—especially when and where cultures overlap.[71] Therefore, the rewriting of a Greco-Roman myth by a Jewish redactor would make a great deal of sense, especially at those historical moments in which tensions were greatest. This does not require us to think of a continual, explicit sectarian mentality. It only requires that one author, at one singular moment in history, found Roman domination and Gentile practices unpalatable enough to challenge their authority by subverting a myth central to Roman propaganda.

THE JEWISH REDACTION
OF THE DRAGON SLAYER MYTH

If the author of Revelation 12 incorporated a Jewish recension of the older Greco-Roman Dragon Slayer myth, can we postulate the elements of such a reconstruction? In her seminal text, *The Combat Myth in the Book of Revelation*, Adela Yarbro Collins offers such a reconstruction— along with the following caution: "The isolation of such material [sources in Revelation 12] is not equivalent to reconstruction of these sources, since certainty about how they began or ended is not attainable."[72] With this caution in mind, I reproduce her reconstruction of the Jewish redaction of the Dragon Slayer myth. (I have left the verse numbers of Revelation 12 intact in order that we might see the uniqueness of this Jewish reconstruction and to assist us later in seeing what the Christian redactor added to this layer.) I will argue later in this chapter that the Christian redactor combined a strictly Jewish text with accounts of the battle in heaven and the dragon's slaying (Rev. 12:7-9), a Christian victory hymn (Rev. 12:10-12), and other editorial additions (vv. 1, 3, 4, 6, 13, and 17). For now, I focus on this Jewish subversion of the Dragon Slayer myth:

> [1][And behold] a woman. [2]She was with child and she cried out in birth pangs, in anguish for delivery. [3][And] behold a great red dragon, with seven heads and ten horns. [4]And the dragon stood before the woman who was about to bear a child, that he might devour her child when she brought it forth; [5]She brought forth a male child, one who is to rule all the nations with a rod of iron, but the child was caught up to God and to his throne. [14]But the woman was given the two wings of the great eagle that she might fly from the serpent into the wilderness, to the place where she is to be nourished for a time, and times, and half a time. [15]The serpent poured water like a river out of his mouth after the woman, to sweep her away with the flood. [16]But the earth came to the help of the woman, and the earth opened its mouth and swallowed the river which the dragon had poured from his mouth.[73]

What value would such a work have for its Jewish author or audience? On this issue, Yarbro Collins contends, "The rule of Augustus was celebrated as a golden age and as the rule of Apollo. The Apollo myth and cult were made to function as political propaganda for the empire. . . . Since Augustus was the model for later emperors, a dissident Jew might express opposition to Rome at any time in the first century by co-opting Apollonian motifs."[74] By extension, a dissident Jew could also express opposition to local leaders, rituals, and communal expectations by adopting such oppositional motifs. However, we should not expect the Jewish adaptation of the Dragon Slayer myth to be a literal, mirror image of its imperial counterpart. What we should expect to see is a reinscribed and coded appropriation of the imperial myth that allows for imperialized readers/hearers to identify the subliminal allusion to the imperial myth while simultaneously recognizing the subversive reinscription of it.

This reinscribing is readily identifiable in the Jewish subversion of the Dragon Slayer myth. The two forms of the myth (Roman and Jewish) both employ a form of the ancient combat myth in which the dragon represents chaos. In the Roman form of the myth, chaos is identified as the shift from republic to empire, with the accompanying civil wars, piracy, and banditry that followed the assassination of Julius Caesar. In the Jewish form of the myth, "the interference of a foreign power [Rome] is expressed as the threat of chaos."[75] Therefore, the original Roman intention of the myth has been simultaneously deflected and subverted by its Jewish (re)interpretation. Rome is the source of political chaos rather than the source of peace (that is, order). In this instance, the ideology of *pax Romana* is critiqued from a non-Roman, imperially marginalized perspective.

The subversion of the Dragon Slayer myth does not end here. The Jewish version of the myth also alters the primary protagonist: Apollo is replaced by the Jewish Messiah. Again, the value of the myth for the empire was that subsequent emperors viewed Apollo as a political archetype and the restorer of the Golden Age. In the Jewish form of the myth, Apollo is replaced by the Messiah via the allusion to Psalm 2:9, a psalm that came to have an explicitly messianic interpretation. According to Aune, "The gloss is intended to identify the male child as the Messiah of Jewish eschatological expectation and to place that rule in the *future*."[76] The future role of the Messiah should not go unnoticed. This helps explain the immediate translation of the Messiah to God in the Jewish form of the myth. An overtly Christian reading would assume that the translation of the Messiah (that is, Christ) occurred after the death and resurrection of Jesus. From a Jewish perspective, however, this translation occurred right after the birth of the Messiah, and this fits well with later rabbinic expectations of the "temporarily hidden messiah."[77] This form of the myth is congruent with later Jewish messianic expectations.

The role of the woman is also analogous to the role of Leto in the Dragon Slayer myth. Both women are pursued by the dragon because of the expected religiopolitical ramifications that would arise with the birth of their offspring. Leto is removed from the threat of the dragon by the wind, which eventually leads her to Neptune for her ultimate care. In the Jewish form of the myth, the wings of an eagle transport the woman to the wilderness, where she is eventually protected by the earth, which swallows the flood waters that spewed out of the mouth of the dragon. In both instances, the primary deities (Yahweh and Zeus/Jove) actively remove the threat of the dragon by transporting the women to new locations, where they are protected by either Neptune or the earth.

What is of greatest import here is not the reconstruction of scene-by-scene analogies of the two versions of the myth but rather echoes and allusions of the Dragon Slayer myth in the reconfigured Jewish countermyth. The most powerful reinscription in this particular subversion of an imperial myth is the replacement of the primary protagonist, Apollo, with the eschatological Jewish Messiah. The bringer of order is not the imperial archetype Apollo, but rather the future Jewish Messiah. From an ideological perspective, this substitution completely undermines the most significant claims of the Dragon Slayer myth in favor of a people who seek cosmic solutions to earthly political realities.

CHRISTIANS IN ASIA MINOR AT THE END OF THE FIRST CENTURY C.E.

Our attention now turns to delimiting the sociopolitical circumstances that served as stimuli and background for the production of the book of Revelation. In *Crisis and Catharsis: The Power of the Apocalypse*, Adela Yarbro Collins offers a textured and in-depth analysis of the situation of Christians in Asia Minor as reflected in the book of Revelation.[78] Rather than a single explanation for the writing of Revelation—namely, widespread imperial persecutions of Christians during the reign of Domitian—she finds a multifaceted occasion, including (1) conflict with

Jews, (2) conflict with Gentiles of Asia Minor, (3) conflict over wealth, and (4) precarious relations with Rome. Her argument is based on the internal evidence of the book of Revelation and offers much insight into why a Jewish Christian scribe would appropriate a Jewish retelling of a Greco-Roman myth. She summarizes these four areas as follows:

CRISIS 1: CONFLICT WITH THE JEWS
The correspondence to the Church at Smyrna reads thus:

> I know your affliction and your poverty, even though you are rich. I know the slander on the part of those who say they are Jews and are not, but are a synagogue of Satan. Do not fear what you are about to suffer. Beware, the devil is about to throw some of you into prison, so that you may be tested, and for ten days you will have affliction. Be faithful until death, and I will give you the crown of life (Rev. 2:9-10).

An initial glance into the Apocalypse reveals that its author is dealing with a multifaceted social crisis well beyond the singular and supposed persecution of Domitian. This first crisis becomes even more complicated with the realization that the city of Jerusalem is presented both as a symbol of salvation (Rev. 21:9-27) and, by way of contrast, in negative terms as Sodom and Egypt (Rev. 11:8) in subsequent chapters. Therefore, it is fair to assume that John's issues with Jewish congregations are localized if not regional, but by no means comprehensive.

Yarbro Collins assesses the situation between Christians and Jews in Asia Minor as follows:

> At first, followers in Jesus and the believers in the Christ considered themselves to be and were perceived by Gentiles as part of that complex diversity we speak of as ancient Judaism. . . . The awareness of difference (between Jew and Christian) probably created a crisis of identity for at least some believers in Christ. It also made the public status of some Christians precarious. There was in the early empire a strong suspicion of new religions. Only those firmly rooted in ethnic tradition and homeland were acceptable. Christians

of course had no ancient tradition, no national identity, and no homeland or religious center besides those of the Jews. . . . Revelation contains evidence that the controversies between the believers in Christ and local Jews had created a social crisis for at least some Christians in Asia Minor.[79]

CRISIS 2: CONFLICT WITH NEIGHBORING GENTILES

The historian Tacitus records that Nero singled out Christians as scapegoats for the fire in Rome because there already existed a widespread animosity against them. Other second-century accusations against the Christians included incest and cannibalism. Yarbro Collins suggests that the most fundamental charge was that of hatred of the human race.[80] She concludes that these accusations, widespread in the second century of the Common Era, were, in fact, already fairly widespread in the first.

These charges are more than likely the result of Christian exclusiveness, which prevented Christians from participating in the public worship of Roman deities. The prohibition of eating meat sacrificed to idols exemplifies this exclusiveness and adds to Christian isolation and Gentile suspicions of this emerging cult.

CRISIS 3: CONFLICT OVER WEALTH

The message to Laodicea is quite explicit about the problems personal wealth is causing in the congregation:

> For you say, "I am rich, I have prospered, and I need nothing." You do not realize that you are wretched, pitiable, poor, blind, and naked. Therefore I counsel you to buy from me gold refined by fire so that you may be rich; and white robes to clothe you and to keep the shame of your nakedness from being seen; and salve to anoint your eyes so that you may see (Rev. 3:17-18).

Likewise, in Revelation 18, Rome is attacked for being the source of wealth:

> "The fruit for which your soul longed has gone from you, and all your dainties and your splendor are lost to you, never to

be found again!" The merchants of these wares, who gained wealth from her, will stand far off, in fear of her torment, weeping and mourning aloud. "Alas, alas, the great city, clothed in fine linen, in purple and scarlet, adorned with gold, with jewels, and with pearls! For in one hour all this wealth has been laid waste" (Rev. 18:14-17).

On this issue, Yarbro Collins suggests that Revelation was written during a time of great social unrest in Asia Minor, an unrest that was fueled primarily by the tension between rich and poor over the issue of social injustice. This thesis agrees with the perspective of Michael Rostovtzoff, Roman social historian, whose analysis of Asian society assumes a model of social conflict based on the acute financial disconnect between elites and non-elites. He argues that class conflict between the poor and wealthy in Asia is one of the crises that inspired the writing of Revelation.[81]

CRISIS 4: PRECARIOUS RELATIONS WITH ROME

Five traumatic events reflected in Revelation point directly to Rome as adversary:

1. The use of the name Babylon for Rome alludes to residual trauma from the destruction of the Jerusalem Temple by Rome in 70 B.C.E.

2. The covert references to Emperor Nero in chapters 11, 13, and 17 as adversary of God and the saints reflect the experience of arrest, conviction, torture, and execution of Christians in Rome at Nero's order.

3. In the message to Pergamum (Rev. 2:12-17), the death of a Christian, Antipas, is explicitly mentioned. In light of chapters 12, 13, and 17, the reference to Satan is a veiled allusion to Roman power.

4. In Revelation 1:9, John says he was on the island of Patmos "because of the word of God and the testimony of Jesus." John, no doubt, is a victim of Roman rule. According to both Tertullian and Jerome, John's case was an example of *relegatio in insulam* (banishment to an island) (Tertullian,

De praescriptione haereticorum 36; Jerome, *De viris illustribus* 9). During the imperial period, *relegatio* was normally a life sentence of banishment for a particular offense or because an individual threatened public interest and security.

5. The last example of Christian trauma reflected in the book of Revelation was the exposure to the imperial cult in Asia Minor. Collins describes the situation in the following manner:

> For some Christians of the first and second centuries . . . the imperial cult must have been deeply offensive. The polytheism with which it was joined was equally distasteful. The imperial cult was enthusiastically supported in Asia Minor, often beyond the expectation of the Roman authorities, and sometimes even in conflict with their sensibilities. The public display must have been traumatic for Christians who opposed its ideology deeply and intensely.[82]

For the monotheistic Christians, the problem of the imperial cult became increasingly acute with the Christian separation from traditional Judaism. Christians were no longer afforded the shelter of being part of an ancient religious and ethnic tradition. The Jews were in a privileged position that the Christians could no longer share.

Yarbro Collins's recognition of these four crises adds texture and depth to our understanding of the historical situation that gave rise to the book of Revelation. Even without the issue of widespread persecutions, the issue of empire is still extremely relevant. Issues of unfair economic practices and imperial worship could still be ultimately attributed directly to Roman governing policies in Asia Minor. Conflicts with neighboring Gentiles can also be framed as being generated by Gentile and Roman expectations of public worship of Roman deities. Jewish and Christian exclusiveness would be seen as suspicious by Gentile neighbors, especially by the elite of Asia Minor who desired to exhibit a positive representation of themselves to Rome. Finally, conflict with the synagogue could also be framed within the Roman imperial context.

Jewish rejection of Christians could mean that Rome would no longer afford Christians certain concessions that they gave to Jews. The tensions and the beginning of the separation of Jews and Christians would leave Christians more vulnerable in relation to Rome.

This tension might, therefore, help explain why a Christian scribe would adopt a Jewish retelling of the Dragon Slayer myth as his moment of subversion. A Christian, by adopting the Jewish redeployment of the Dragon Slayer myth, could simultaneously critique the Roman Empire— again by subverting Apollonian motifs—and also the Jewish authorities who first cast this story in Jewish terms.

CHRISTIAN REDACTION OF THE JEWISH SOURCE

I now discuss the phenomenon of the Christian redaction of the Jewish version of the Dragon Slayer myth that led to the creation of Revelation 12.[83] I argue that all additions made to the Jewish source (as reconstructed on pp. 40–41) were contributed by Christian redactors at the end of the first century C.E. Although such reconstructions are at best educated estimations of these sources, since we have no way of being certain of the actual shape of these texts, they nevertheless allow us to see much more clearly the redeployment and recontextualizations associated with the earlier form of the myth. Once the reconstructions are established, I offer the rationale for such redeployments.

The Jewish redaction of the Dragon Slayer myth that serves as the primary source for Revelation 12 is reconstructed earlier in this chapter (p. 32). Most scholars of Revelation 12 recognize that, in addition to this source, a second Jewish source has been conflated into this literary scenario by a Christian redactor. This reconstructed source is similar to texts in the Hebrew Bible such as Psalm 74, Isaiah 27, and Daniel 8, all of which depict the rebellion of Satan in heaven. This source has been reconstructed by Yarbro Collins as follows (again I maintain the verse numbers of Revelation 12 for comparative convenience):

> [7]And a war broke out in heaven; Michael and his angels fighting against [Satan], and [Satan] and his angels fought back. [8]But they were defeated and there was no longer any place for them

in heaven. [9]And [Satan] was thrown down to the earth and his angels were thrown down with him (Rev. 12:7-9).[84]

With the two Jewish sources in place, what is left over in Revelation 12 can be attributed to the creative energies of the Christian redactor. The overall redactional activity of Revelation 12 can be mapped out, therefore, as follows:

1. Jewish Source I, created by a Jewish author to subvert the Dragon Slayer myth (vv. 1-5, 14-16)
2. Jewish Source II, independently created by a Jewish author and integrated into Jewish Source I by a Christian redactor for Revelation 12 (vv. 7-9)
3. Christian Victory Hymn, appended to Jewish Source II (vv. 10-12)
4. Christian redactions/additions to Jewish Source I (partial additions in vv. 1, 3, and 4; full-verse additions of vv. 6, 13, and 17)
5. Christian redactions/additions to Jewish Source II (substitution of Satan for dragon in v. 7; partial addition in v. 9)

There is no way to posit that these additions took place in stages. Affirming that they did would also not enhance my argument with respect to the subversion of the Dragon Slayer myth. As I argue in the discussion that follows, the totality of these additions is what makes the most "subversive sense."

The first addition to these two Jewish sources is the "Christian Victory Hymn," which is appended to Jewish Source II and equivalent to Revelation 12:10-12:

[10]And I heard a loud voice in heaven saying, "Now the salvation and the power and the kingdom of our God and the authority of his Christ have come, for the accuser of our brethren has been thrown down, who accuses them day and night before our God. [11]And they have conquered him by the blood of the Lamb and by the word of their testimony, for they loved not their lives even unto death. [12]Rejoice, then, O heaven and you that dwell within! But woe to you, O earth

and sea, for the devil has come down to you in great wrath, because he knows that his time is short!"[85]

The final redactional activity that must be accounted for in Revelation 12 consists of the additions made to the two Jewish sources. For the sake of clarity, the first set of additions will be referred to as "Christian additions/redactions to Source I" and is reconstructed as follows:

> [1]And a great sign appeared in heaven . . . clothed with the sun, with the moon under her feet, and on her head a crown of twelve stars.
>
> [3]And another sign appeared in heaven; . . . and seven diadems upon his heads.
>
> [4]His tail swept down a third of the stars in heaven, and cast them to the earth.
>
> [6]And the woman fled to the wilderness, where she has a place prepared by God, in which to be nourished for one thousand two hundred and sixty days.
>
> [13]And when the dragon saw that he had been thrown down to the earth, he pursued the woman who had borne the male child.
>
> [17]Then the dragon was angry with the woman, and went off to make war on the rest of her offspring, on those who keep the commandments of God and bear testimony to Jesus. And he stood on the sand of the sea.[86]

The second set of additions, "Christian redaction/additions to Source II," includes the following verses:

> [7]. . . [dragon: replaces Satan in original Jewish source]; . . . [dragon] . . . .
>
> [9]And the great dragon . . . that ancient serpent, who is called the devil and Satan, the deceiver of the whole world, he was thrown down.[87]

With John the prophet's editorial additions accounted for, we can now focus on his strategy of appropriating and subverting the Dragon Slayer myth for the benefit of his marginalized Christian perspective.

ANALYSIS AND JUSTIFICATION
OF CHRISTIAN REDACTION IN REVELATION 12

The Christian use of Jewish Source I can easily be extrapolated by recognizing that the Christian seer still saw himself and his movement as part of that ancient tradition known as Judaism or, more specifically, diaspora Judaism. His extensive employment of the Hebrew Bible, the multiple references to Jerusalem (both positive and negative), and his chastisement of the synagogues in Smyrna and Philadelphia are tinged with language of infighting rather than a general sense of anti-Judaism. Therefore, John's incorporation of Jewish Source I is not an adaptation and subversion of a Jewish myth against Judaism but rather the redeployment of a myth borrowed from the sibling religion in hopes of arguing his case as the true tradent of messianic Judaism within the context of empire. As a result, the polemic against Rome that the original author of Jewish Source I employed is still valid for this Christian Jew, who would reconfigure it at the end of the first century of the Common Era. Yarbro Collins supports this thesis by recognizing that the background to both Jewish Source I and Revelation 12 is the domination of the East by Rome.

From a Jewish Christian perspective, the critique of imperial Rome employed by the Jewish author of Source I was still valid in his time. Not only could a practitioner of Judaism adduce Apollonian motifs to critique the emperor in the first century, but so too could a Christian scribe. Jewish Source I provided a fertile starting point for this Christian redactor to amplify this shrouded critique of emperor and Rome.

Why, then, was Jewish Source II appended to Source I? How does it function within the context of Revelation 12? According to Yarbro Collins, Source II brings to a conclusion what was expected and never achieved in Source I, namely, the defeat of the dragon. She argues for this expectation based on her work on combat motifs of the ancient Near East.[88] This is also what would be expected if one adheres to Hyginus's version of the Dragon Slayer myth. Ultimately, the dragon must be defeated. This motif does not occur in Jewish Source I; rather, the Jewish author leaves his readers to extrapolate this expectation from Jewish messianic mythologies and a direct allusion to Psalm 2. With the inclusion of Jewish Source II, the Christian redactor leaves little to speculation. In his rendering of the text, the dragon is defeated in the heavenly battle with Michael and the other angels. It is a Christian recasting of an ancient cosmology with an ethical dimension that accounts for the present situation in which humans must align themselves with either good or evil.[89]

The Victory Hymn, found in Revelation 12:10-12, provides commentary for the battle in heaven and the casting out of Satan from heaven found in verses 7-9. The hymn offers validation for the defeat of the Satan in the heavenly realms and clearly defines the ultimate protagonist and antagonist in this apocalyptic drama. It is not Michael and the angels positioned against Satan. Rather, there is a heightening in the stakes of the battle. Ultimately, it is the Lamb and God who are Satan's archrivals and tormentors in this movement. The Victory Hymn also sets up the battle that will continue on earth between Satan and the woman and her offspring.

The Christian additions to Jewish Source I are extensive. On this matter Yarbro Collins observes that

> the narrative of the woman and the dragon [Jewish Source I] was composed as a figurative representation of political-religious conflict in which the opponent was cast in the role of the chaos-beast. In the [Christian] redaction, the process of mythicization is taken one step further. The new heavenly setting contributes to this intensification, in that the story of the conflict is removed from the specifically political realm.[90]

What is this Christian intensification of Jewish Source I, and what purpose does it serve? First, the conflict between the woman and the dragon as it appears in Jewish Source I had an earthly setting in the form that I have projected. The Christian redactor, incorporating it into a vision account, moves the action of the conflict into the heavenly realms (for example, "And a great sign appeared in heaven, a woman"). This is also supported by his conflation of Source I with Source II, the Battle in Heaven. If Satan is cast out of heaven in Source II, he must have been there in Source I.

At this point, asking this question is necessary: What is Leto doing in the heavenly realm since she is never positioned there in the Dragon Slayer myth? Commentators on Revelation have long argued that the heavenly woman in Revelation 12 is *either* Leto or Isis. With the introduction of the Jewish layer into the discussion, however, it can compellingly be argued that the woman in this early layer is Leto because of the terrestrial setting of the story. But now I must account for the heavenly imagery introduced or overlaid onto this Jewish layer. Who is this heavenly woman clothed in the sun, standing on the moon and wearing a crown of stars? After an analysis of heavenly female figures in Roman antiquity, Yarbro Collins concludes that this change can be directly attributed to the overlaying of *heavenly* Isis imagery onto the woman of Jewish Source I:[91]

> In Revelation 12 then we seem to have a *fusing* of Leto and Isis traditions. Such a combination is not surprising since analogous birth stories were associated with the two goddesses. The narrative of ch. 12 reflects the pattern of these myths, particularly the pattern of the Leto myth. The description of the [heavenly] woman reflects the typical image of Isis.

If, indeed, the narrative of chapter 12 reflects the pattern of the Leto myth, we can conclude that the anti-Roman overtones originally found in Jewish Source I are still valid from a Christian perspective. What must be accounted for is the importation of Isis imagery into this narrative. If the original source for the Christian redactor was Jewish Source I, which in my reconstructed form made no allusion to the heavenly realm, it can be argued that the Isis imagery shifts and intensifies the battle between the dragon and the woman (and her offspring) into the heavenly realm. Again, according to Yarbro Collins, "Thus the use of the vision form may have contributed to the transformation of the characters in the narrative from metaphors for earthly realities to heavenly beings."[92] The human and earthly bound Leto of the original Dragon Slayer myth has been promoted to the heavenly realms by the intentional superimposition of the heavenly Isis onto Leto's initial mundane character.

It should, therefore, not surprise us that the Christian additions to Jewish Source II would include a replacement of Satan with a dragon, thus aligning and equating it with the dragon in Jewish Source I, while simultaneously defining exactly who the dragon is in Sources I and II:

"And the great dragon . . . that ancient serpent, who is called the Devil and Satan, the deceiver of the whole world—he was thrown down." With the additions to sources I and II, the Christian redactor of chapter 12 changes the realm of the earthly religiopolitical overtones of Source I into the precursor for the final heavenly eschatological battle between Satan and the Lamb. The Christian drama imposed no boundaries on this battle; therefore, "the reinterpretation of the dragon spiritualizes and universalizes his conflict with the woman. The issue is no longer a nationalistic one with cosmic overtones, but one which has to do with the fundamentally dualistic nature of reality."[93]

CONCLUSION

Jews and Christians in Asia Minor shared one striking sociocultural and religiopolitical reality in the first century of the Common Era: the domination of the East by Rome. As our reconstruction of the Jewish and Christian situations in Asia Minor has demonstrated, both groups found themselves in some degree of conflict with Rome. For the Jews, it was the conflict with neighboring Gentiles over how to participate in the provincial and regional representation of power in the form of the emerging imperial cult. In much the same manner, the Christians struggled with their Gentile neighbors over issues of cultic representation and participation but also—according to the internal evidence of Revelation—faced isolated persecutions, economic hardships, recollection of the destruction of the Jerusalem Temple, and issues of assimilation. And like the Jews, the author of Revelation ultimately framed these issues by locating their genesis and impetus in Rome. The Christian author was even so bold as to suggest—albeit in coded language—that Rome and the emperor were one of the two beasts that ultimately derived their power from Satan.[94] Both instances—the Jewish and Christian subversions of the Dragon Slayer and Subjugator myths—are prime examples of those on the margins who write back at and signify against the center.

My primary thesis is that people living on the margins of power, especially those who find themselves in imperial, colonial, and neocolonial contexts will challenge centers of power in patterned ways over both time and culture. One such example of this challenge is the subversion of the imperial myths used to justify and maintain such claims to power. The Dragon Slayer myth was one mythic example used to justify Roman imperial claims to power. Apollo, the prototypical emperor, would establish the Golden Age of Rome in which all subsequent emperors would model and justify their reign. This assertion is well established in the histories and archaeology of antiquity. Subjects of the empire were well aware of the power of this mythical motif and understood that effective diatribes against emperor and empire could very well begin with critique of one of its foundational myths. This was certainly the case on at least two occasions for a Jewish and a Christian scribe in the early imperial era. The genius of these two adaptations is that they both employ important aspects of imperial propaganda in a completely subversive way. The Jewish author replaces the role of Apollo by inserting the Jewish Messiah as the protagonist. The Christian author raises the ante by suggesting that Jesus Christ specifically assumes the role of protagonist; he amplifies his argument by incorporating the heavenly imagery of the Greco-Roman Dragon Subjugator so as to move the conflict from the realm of the earthly and political to a heightened cosmic struggle between the Lamb of God and Satan.

CHAPTER 2

SUBVERTING A *CONQUISTA* MYTH IN SEVENTEENTH-CENTURY MEXICO: THE VIRGIN OF GUADALUPE

MEDIEVAL SPAIN AND SPANISH CATHOLICISM

AN UNDERSTANDING OF THE CREOLE (*criollo*)[1] subversion of the myth of the Virgin of Guadalupe, which the Spanish brought to the Americas, requires a brief review of medieval Spanish history as it relates to the Guadalupe tradition. Analyses of preconquest Mexico are also necessary because it is on this stage that the Spanish conquistadors arrived and continued the policies developed during the *reconquista* (reconquest; see p. 48 below). Also, on this stage, a developing sense of rivalry was cultivated between the Spaniards and the Creoles of the Americas. And finally, this is the period from which the first known documents of the Marian apparition in the Americas are attested. The first of these documents advocated for the Creoles, and the second advocated for the indigenous inhabitants of this "new world."

To speak of a singular Spain at the moment of its first cross-Atlantic explorations in 1492 is at best a gross anachronism. The Iberian Peninsula in 1492 is most accurately described as a loose confederation of states comprising the regions of Navarre, Castile-León, Aragon, Portugal, and Granada.[2] The marriage in 1469 of Fernando, heir to the throne of Aragon, and Isabel, heir to the throne of Castile, marked the beginning of the unification of what would come to be known as the modern state of Spain although through the sixteenth century, it was common to refer to each region as an individual political identity or collectively as the "Spains."[3] The region of Castile-León "held the monopoly on New World discovery, conquests, and government, [so] its impact was the greatest."[4] Any description of the entity that brought Christianity to the New World should, therefore, be viewed in this light. "It was not Spain that undertook the discovery and conquest of the New World but the kingdom of Castile,"[5] under the direction and reign of Fernando and Isabel.

A second component in the reconstruction of medieval Spanish history is the Muslim occupation of the bulk of the Iberian Peninsula between the years 711 and 1492. In 711, a dispatch of Arabic-Islamic nomads, commonly labeled with the pejorative Western term *Moors*, crossed the Strait of Gibraltar from the north of Africa into the Iberian Peninsula.[6] Within a period of seven years, these nomads controlled most of the peninsula, with the exception of the northeast. In light of these military campaigns and subsequent territorial occupations by the Arabic colonizers, the *reconquista* loosely signifies the period of Spanish history in which Iberians—who self-identified not as Spaniards nor as residents of their specific states, but as Christians—attempted to expel the Arabic-Islamic nomads from the Iberian peninsula.[7] This period was extremely formative in the construction of the religious and political identity that Spain would export to the Americas. It has been described as the historical process that most acutely defined the "Spanish character and mentality, both in myth and reality. Militant religiosity, individualism, courage, fatalism, stoicism, arrogance, ethnocentrism, nationalism, a strong sense of personal honor (*pundonor*), and the use of force for religious ends were the heritage of this last great European crusade."[8]

This emergence of a collective "Spanish" identity occurred concurrently with the development of a state-church under the reign of Fernando and Isabel, a relationship sometimes referred to as the *patronato real* (the right of royal patronage). The *patronato* presupposed that churches were supported (and manipulated) most effectively by political endowments rather than by donations from the faithful. During the sixteenth century, it had become a common practice for households to endow churches in return for pastoral positions for family members. Under the reign of Fernando and Isabel, this system of patronage emerged into a national system.[9] In the second half of the sixteenth century, the *patronato* was more widespread and more strictly practiced in the Americas than in the regions of Spain. Its practice became so widespread, and the governmental control over the church so institutionalized, that Spanish Catholicism during the early years of the conquest could be categorized as a national church.

Also formative during medieval Spanish history was the rise of the Spanish Inquisition. Founded in the year 1480 at the request of Fernando and Isabel, the Inquisition was the papal and Spanish "examination" of the sincerity of recent Christian converts. Along with the increase of anti-Semitic and anti-Muslim acts on the peninsula, especially between 1391 and 1492, Jews and Muslims were required to convert to Christianity. Converts from Judaism were known as *conversos*, and from Islam, as *moriscos*. During the fifteenth and sixteenth centuries, many *conversos* landed prominent positions in religious orders and in the church in general. Because of their large numbers and high ranks, the *conversos* aroused ecclesiastical and political suspicions that they were a threat to the very notion of Spanish religious orthodoxy—a sentiment no doubt fueled by the centuries-long *reconquista* mentality.

A by-product of the Spanish Inquisition was the development of the notion of "purity of blood." As with the Inquisition, the issue of purity of blood was a strategy to unify the Iberian Peninsula under the control of the crown of Castile in religious terms. The state sought to identify those individuals whose Christian lineage was "scarred" by having *converso* or *morisco* blood in their immediate ancestry (new Christians). When exported to the Americas, this concept was transferred to individuals who were "contaminated" by either Indian or African ancestry and were consequently refused the right to hold higher political positions. In the Americas, purity of blood was a major consideration in the distribution of appointments to offices in the Spanish churches.[10] In this way, foreign-born Spaniards or Creoles were relegated to second-class citizenship, being excluded from holding prestigious and powerful political and religious positions.

Also within the realm of religious practice and ideology, a twelfth-century Italian theologian, Joachim of Fiore (d. 1202), was particularly influential in the evolution of mystical strains of medieval Spanish thought. A medieval mystic, Joachim strongly influenced the sense of destiny and providence that would flourish under the Franciscans, the Spanish monarchy, and Christopher Columbus in medieval Spain. Joachim postulated three major epochs in human history.[11] The period from Adam to Jesus Christ, he maintained, was that of God the Father and the Hebrew Scriptures and was considered the layperson's church. The period from Jesus to 1260 (the period in which Joachim himself lived) was that of God the Son, the Christian Testament, and the papal church. The final period was to begin in 1260 and would be the age of the Holy Spirit. More significantly, this third epoch would correspond to the friars' church (undoubtedly, the reason why the Franciscans looked so favorably upon the prophecies of Joachim). This epoch, according to Joachim, was the age of the new millennial kingdom, based on his interpretation of the Apocalypse of John.

This interpretation would have major implications for the framing of Spanish notions of "manifest destiny" in the Americas and their readings of the Apocalypse:

> [The third epoch] was to be inaugurated by a new Adam or a new Christ *who would be the founder of a new monastic order.* The transition between the Papal Church of the second age and the Spiritual Church of the third age would be a time of great troubles during which the period of the Papal Church was to endure all the sufferings that corresponded to Christ's passion. The Papal Church would be resurrected as the Spiritual Church in which all men would live the contemplative life, practice apostolic poverty, and enjoy angelic natures. To this level Joachim's ideas were debased and popularized during the thirteenth century by a series of pseudo-Joachimite writings, *which probably originated amongst the spiritual Franciscans themselves. St. Francis was identified with the Messiah that Joachim prophesied.* During the later Middle Ages Joachinism and the Apocalypse preserved their ideological union.[12]

This expectation of the dawn of the final epoch of human history, together with the mendicant Messiah, was of particular and timely interest to the Franciscans, whose founder, Francis of Assisi (ca. 1181–1226) was a contemporary of Joachim. As I point out later in this chapter, the

Franciscans were central figures in the evangelization of the Americas. By framing their mission along the lines of Joachimite prophecy, they made themselves major players in the apocalyptic drama that was unfolding in the Americas. In their worldview, the discovery of the Americas was the final chapter of human history, as they understood it to be revealed in Matthew 28:19-20, where Jesus says, "Go therefore and make disciples of all nations, baptizing them in the name of the Father and of the Son and of the Holy Spirit, and teaching them to obey everything that I have commanded you. And remember, I am with you always, to the end of the age."

With the arrival of twelve Spanish Franciscans in Mexico in 1524, the Franciscans were the first mendicants to come to the Americas. They had inherited an acute millenarian sense of destiny via their founder, Francis of Assisi, who himself was profoundly influenced by the millennial prophecies of Joachim.[13] They understood themselves as the primary protagonists in the drama that was initiated with the discovery of a new land and by people who required Christian conversion as the prologue to the long-awaited Parousia.

The apocalyptic expectation and sense of destiny imported from the Old to the New World has been described as "the first manifestation of the Creole spirit in America."[14] This was the direct result of the subversion of Spaniard messianic expectations that were accompanied by their sense of destiny that had been developed during the *reconquista*:[15]

> In this climate of providential exaltation and messianic expectation was born a Franciscan current which nourished the Creole mentality of New Spain. In the conception of the Franciscan pioneers, this New Spain was to be as radically new in relation to traditional Spain as the new church was to be in respect to the Roman church. The first missionaries of Mexico were certainly "Creoles" in the measure that they wanted to create a new world, which implied rupture with the Old.[16]

This apocalyptic worldview and sense of divine providence were not limited to the mendicants. The Spanish monarchy was also understood in Joachimite terms and as such was considered a coparticipant in this final eschatological epoch. Genónimo de Mendieta, O.F.M., a sixteenth-century Franciscan mendicant friar (1525–1604), maintained that the Spanish race under the guidance of the monarchy had been selected to convert Jews, Muslims, and other non-Christians—an event that foreshadowed the imminent apocalypse:[17]

> God had raised Spain above all of the kingdoms of the earth, and He had designated the Spaniards as His new chosen people. . . . During the Middle Ages one important aspect of the theory of Christian kingship was the apostolic idea; that one duty of the king was to spread the gospel among the heathen. In the Middle Ages all kings were regarded as missionary kings, as apostle-like kings.[18]

This sense of mission and destiny was a vital component of Fernando and Isabel's understandings of their role as sovereigns of the emerging Spanish empire.

Jacques Lafaye argues that the confusion of the realms of religion and politics was a direct result of this eschatological conception of history that was commonplace in Europe for centuries.[19] Spanish Christians, the new chosen people, were envisaged as taking on the task of making Christianity truly catholic through the conversion of non-Christians, Muslims, and by leading apostate Jews back into the Christian fold. In this worldview, "The monarchs were charged with the Christianization of the peoples of these newly discovered lands."[20] Consequently, the task of the "chosen" (Spanish) Christian, whether a monarch, a religious leader, an explorer, or other, was to hasten the coming of this messianic era by means of the close scrutiny of Scripture, in particular the book of Revelation, and the evangelization of both Old and New World peoples.

The possibility of evangelizing New World peoples came on October 12, 1492, with the "discovery" of the Americas by a Genoese sailor named Christopher Columbus. Columbus had been commissioned by Fernando and Isabel to search out alternative trade routes to the East since traditional land routes had been closed off by Muslims in the regions of East Central Asia. Like the Franciscans who would come after him, Columbus would also frame his explorations through the lens of apocalyptic prophecy. Like other mystical exegetes of his day, Columbus was firmly convinced that the world was rapidly approaching its end. He estimated that only one hundred and fifty years remained. . . . But before the awesome event could come to pass, all prophecies had to be filled. The gospel had to be preached to all peoples and to all races and in all tongues . . . . Little wonder that he was obsessed with the image of himself as an instrument of Divine Providence.[21]

Columbus's frame of reference was indebted to the Spiritual Franciscan tradition, the mendicant order that was most accommodating to this apocalyptic worldview.[22] In a well-circulated story, Columbus, after his second voyage to the Americas, returned to Spain and appeared in the streets of Seville, dressed in sackcloth as a penitent Franciscan. At critical moments in his career, the Franciscans extended much-needed support to Columbus, and in return, Columbus was partial to the Franciscans. The extent to which Columbus adhered to the mystical religious framework of the Franciscan order should, therefore, come as no surprise. Both Columbus and the Franciscans were influenced by Joachim of Fiore, as Francis himself had been. As a result, "Columbus linked the crusading tradition to an apocalyptic vision with himself cast in the role of [Joachim's] messiah. . . . The discovery of the Indies, the conversion of all the gentiles, and the deliverance of the Holy Sepulcher were considered to be the three climactic events which would foreshadow the end of the world."[23]

In sum, the Spanish Catholicism that came to the Americas had a distinctively apocalyptic aura. The conflation of a *reconquista* collective identity and Joachimite eschatology infiltrated the mind-sets of politicos and religious and lay peoples alike throughout medieval Spain. With the conquest of the Muslim-held areas, the expulsion of Jews and Muslims from the peninsula, the rise of a monarchy that would begin to unify the states of Spain, and the discovery of the Americas, it is not difficult to imagine how the Spanish people of that time could interpret the unfolding of Spanish history within an apocalyptic framework. The prophecies of Joachim, so influential on Francis, the Franciscans, the monarchy, and Columbus, would have a profound impact on the Spanish Christianity that came to the Americas. Many persons believed that these events, especially the discoveries of Columbus and subsequent explorers, marked the beginning of the end times and would facilitate the rupture between the Old and the New World.

THE MEDIEVAL SPANISH GUADALUPE MYTH

It should also come as no surprise that European apparition accounts would come to the Americas and be interpreted through the lens of Joachimite eschatology. For my purposes, the most notable of these accounts involves the appearance of the Virgin of Guadalupe.

The meaning of the name *Guadalupe* has been debated for centuries. It is generally agreed that the prefix, *guad-*, is a topographic term, probably Arabic, that refers to small bodies of water, such as streams and/or rivers. The remainder of the word, the suffix, is much more problematic. Lafaye has delineated the most popular explanations.[24] The first possibility is that the suffix is derived from the Latin root *lup-*, "wolf," thus rendering the entire word as "River of Wolves." However, Lafaye considers the association of an Arabic radical with a Latin suffix unlikely. He proposes, instead, that *-al-* is the Arabic article, thus rendering "*guad al upe*" or its Spanish equivalent, *rio oculto*, best translated as "river flowing between the high banks." Whether Guadalupe is rendered as "river of wolves" or "river flowing between the high banks," it is agreed that the Virgin received her name from the geographical location in which the national shrine to Our Lady of Guadalupe was built and where she has been venerated for centuries.

The Jeronymites became the earliest and most detailed chroniclers of the Spanish Guadalupan apparition myth in fifteenth-century Spain as a result of their relationship with the national shrine. In 1340, as a response to the momentous *reconquista* victory in the city of Salado, King Alfonso XI ordered the construction of this Gothic church. In 1389, King Juan I requested that the order of Jeronymites would oversee its daily activities and rituals. The Jeronymite monks inhabited the sanctuary from 1389 to 1835.

By consulting the work of Fray Arcangel Barrado Manzano, Lafaye was able to posit the chronological order of the earliest sources concerning the apparition tradition in Spain:

1. *Codex written before 1400,* missing
2. *Codex 555 of the Archivo Histórico Nacional,* written in 1440
3. *Codex of Father Alonso de la Rambla* (1484)
4. *Codex 344 of the Archivo Histórico Nacional,* written in 1500
5. *Codex of Father Diego de Ecija* (died 1534)
6. *Codex of Father Juan Herrera, in the Library of the Escorial, IV-a-10,* written in 1535[25]

As the list indicates, there are several early sources for the Marian/ Guadalupan apparitions. Their contents are quite consistent with other apparition accounts popular in the medieval West, especially in Spain.[26]

Traditional apparition accounts generally included the following components: "a pious image hidden in the mountain; an apparition witnessed by a shepherd, coming at a time when Christians were in dire need of a manifestation of God and his supernatural grace."[27] The apparition account preserved by the Jeronymite monks is consistent with this description. In Codex 555, the earliest of all the available Jeronymite documents, the origin of the statuette of Virgin with child is described as follows:

> At that time (the eighth century) all the Christians fled from Seville. Among them were some saintly priests who took with them the statue of Our Lady, Holy Mary . . . , and in these mountains these priests dug a cave that they surrounded with large gravestones; inside they placed the statue of Our Lady, Holy Mary, together with a small bell and a reliquary containing a writing which told how this statue of Holy Mary had been offered at Rome to the archbishop of Seville, Saint Leander, by the Doctor of the Church, Saint Gregory.[28]

Contemporary legend embellishes this account by adding that the "dark" Virgin (see Appendix Plate 1) and the infant Jesus were originally carved by Saint Luke, buried in Byzantium, discovered, and brought to Pope Gregory the Great in Rome. After the arrival of the statue in Rome, it is attributed with the expulsion of a plague and later transferred to Spain to expel another plague in Seville. Legend also reports that the statue was subsequently buried in the eighth century during the occupation of Spain by the Arabic-Islamic nomads.[29]

A cursory analysis of Codex 555 allows for a reconstruction of the rudimentary features of the Guadalupan tradition as maintained by the fifteenth-century Jeronymites:

> At the time when King Alfonso reign over Spain, Our Lady, the Holy Virgin Mary, appeared to a shepherd in the mountains of Guadalupe. . . . She said to the shepherd: "Have no fear, for I am the Mother of God, through whom mankind will be redeemed. . . ." The shepherd came home, found his wife in tears, and said to her: "Why do you weep?" She replied, "Your son is dead," and he said: "Have no care, for I dedicate him to Holy Mary of Guadalupe, that she may bring him back to life and health." . . . Immediately the young man rose up sound and well; he said to his father: "Father, hasten; let us go to Holy Mary of Guadalupe," at which all who were present marveled. This shepherd went to find the priests and told them . . . that the miracles to be worked by the Virgin would cause many pilgrims from many regions to come to her sanctuary, and that a large village would arise in the great mountain. As soon as the priests and the other people heard that, they set to work.[30]

Preliminary analysis of the documents and traditions surrounding the Spanish Guadalupan tradition raises several relevant issues. First, as maintained in Codex 555 fol. 6v., the hiding of the sacred icon is directly related to the occupation of the Iberian Peninsula by the invading Arabic-Islamic nomads. This aspect is also developed in the Codex of Father Diego de Ecija (early sixteenth century): "After the sword of the Moor had passed through almost all Spain, it pleased God, Our Lord, to comfort the Christians so they might regain the courage they had lost."[31]

Second, the occupation was severe enough to force the Christian population of Seville to flee their city. These two observations directly link the developing Guadalupan tradition with both the occupation of

Spain by Muslims and the incorporation of Guadalupe in the emerging spirit of the *reconquista* in Spain. As noted earlier in this chapter, the sanctuary in Guadalupe was built "as a thanksgiving for the victory at Salado" in 1340.[32] It is clear that the Guadalupan tradition matured simultaneously with the developing spirit of *reconquista* in Spain. The Virgin of Guadalupe was seen as defender and liberator of the Spanish people and their territory against the occupying Muslim colonizers.

In the late fifteenth century, her role in the *reconquista* mentality of Spain became even more explicit with her adoption into the inquisitorial persecution of the *conversos*. The Guadalupan tradition evolved from a posture of defense against the Muslims to an aggressive ideological and political *reconquista* policy against all non-Catholics on the peninsula and eventually in the Americas.

PRECONQUEST MEXICO AND AZTEC RELIGION

Civilization in Mexico began in approximately 1300 B.C.E. in the region of the Gulf Coast called La Venta (modern-day Veracruz) with a people called the Olmecs. Although very little is known of the Olmecs, their civilization is renowned for its stone sculptures and complex calendar system. The Olmecs also built ceremonial cities, pyramids, and temples. The primary deity of the Olmecs was Tlaloc, god of rain, to whom they made human sacrifices. The language of the Olmecs was most probably an early form of Nahuatl, the language that would be spoken in subsequent centuries by the Aztecs. Upon the decline of the Olmec civilization, several locales continued to thrive, among them Teotihuacán (meaning "the place where the gods meet") just to the north of present-day Mexico City; Albán in the Zapotec region, the Huastec region to the northeast of Mexico City, and the Mayan region in modern Guatemala.[33]

The locale most important for my purposes is Teotihuacán because it was the region the Aztecs would ultimately settle and the place where they would encounter the "explorers" from the Old World. After the reign of the Olmecs, the region of Teotihuacán underwent many changes. Like other regions of the Central Plateau, Teotihuacán was conquered on various occasions by wandering tribes from the north. Of these, the most prominent to settle there in the ninth century were the Toltecs. The Toltec capitol, Tollan, became a legendary locale, and the inhabitants of this city were considered masters of architecture, art, and technology.[34]

The primary deity of the Toltecs was the famed Quetzalcóatl, who was viewed as a benevolent deity. Quetzalcóatl was opposed in the Toltec pantheon by Tezcatlipoca, an aggressive god who required human sacrifice. According to ancient Toltec mythology, Tezcatlipoca arranged Quetzalcóatl's downfall, flight from the capital city of Tollan, and move to the east. This myth is significant in Aztec history because, according to report, the Aztec emperor Moctezuma II was instructed by a prophecy of his chief priests that the encroaching Spanish armies signified the return of Quetzalcóatl, marking the downfall of the Aztec empire.[35]

The many wandering tribes that came to Teotihuacán included the Mexica (later known as the Aztecs), who originated from the semilegendary land of Aztlán. Around the thirteenth century, the Mexica left Aztlán and began a series of southern migrations, led by their primary deity Huitzilopochtli, another deity associated with human sacrifice. The Mexica arrived in the Valley of Mexico around the turn of the fourteenth century and became vassals to the local elite.

Forced from one region of the Valley of Mexico to others, the Mexica in 1322 ultimately came to the location that had been prophesied to them by Huitzilopochtli through the priestly class. In that prophetic vision they witnessed an eagle devouring a serpent on a prickly pear cactus (this triad of eagle, serpent, and cactus would eventually become the national symbol of modern Mexico). The place they had come to was an island called Tenochtitlán, a location of strategic military importance. By the end of the fourteenth century, the wandering tribe that was once a vassal people emerged into the dominant political and military force in the region. By 1372, "the simple tribal government was replaced with a monarchy."[36] Scholars offer the following description:

> The Mexica empire took its clear shape toward the end of the fifteenth century. It was not an empire in the modern sense but rather a confederation of three city-states: Tenochtitlán, Texcoco, and Tlacopan. The Mexica, of course were dominant. . . . Tenochtitlán grew into a magnificent city connected to the mainland by causeways and aqueducts.

Dominating its center was the temple to Huitzilopochtli, perched atop an awesome pyramid. At its dedication in 1487 from eight thousand to twenty thousand victims were sacrificed. The city was clean, far more than any contemporary European city, but was subject to flooding from the lakes. In 1519, when Fernando Cortés made his appearance at Veracruz, the Emperor was Moctezuma II Xocoyotzin ("the younger")—ruthless, devious, superstitious, and ultimately tragic.[37]

The religious practices of the Mexica that the Spaniards first encountered in 1519 most likely had evolved from the hybrid nature of their complex polytheism. The Mexica had developed the practice of adopting the deities of the peoples they conquered.[38] This facilitated the incorporation of both male and female deities into their pantheon. In fact, in the religious practices of the indigenous peoples who inhabited the Central Valley of Mexico, most deities had an opposite gender counterpart. This concept, known as *Ometéotl*, depicted the dual nature of the Supreme Being (*Ometecuhtli-Omecíhuatl*) and most other deities in the Mexica pantheon. The feminine aspect of the gods was not a foreign concept to the Mexica but was ingrained in the most rudimentary forms of their religiosity. This would have important implications for the way the Mexica and vassal tribes would be evangelized by the Spaniards.

CONQUEST OF MEXICO AND IMPORTATION OF THE GUADALUPAN CULT

The Spanish sense of *reconquista* was not diminished with expulsion of the Muslims from the Iberian Peninsula in 1492 but was seamlessly extended to the Americas in the early sixteenth century. From the very beginnings of their expeditions, Spanish conquistadors energetically transferred the spirit of the *reconquista* to the New World. The new peoples with their foreign culture, language, and belief systems must be purged and purified, just as the *moriscos* and the *conversos* had been on the peninsula.

In 1516, the Cuban governor, Diego Velasquez, began to send naval expeditions to the east coast of Mexico. In 1519, Velasquez became weary of the highly motivated young mayor of Santiago and accomplished sailor, Hernán Cortés, and sought ways to replace this ambitious young rival. Fearing the loss of his wealth in Cuba and the wealth he anticipated reaping in future expeditions, Cortés set sail for the east coast of Mexico and, in 1519, founded the city of Veracruz, proclaiming himself mayor. Within two years, Hernán Cortés would claim for himself and for the state-church of Spain all rights and privileges of the Mexica empire.

From the very beginning of the conquest of Mexico, the Spanish conquistadors viewed Mary in the form of the Virgin of Guadalupe and her accomplice, the Virgin of Remedios (see pp. 67–8 and 79–81 below), as their advocates. Many of these conquistadors came from the southwest region of Spain known as Estremadura, the location of the national shrine to the Spanish Guadalupe (see Plate 1 in Appendix). Probably, many of the earliest conquistadors were at least knowledgeable about this Spanish pilgrimage site; more likely, they were devotees of the Virgin of Guadalupe. Spanish records from New Spain attest to the belief among these men that, along with James, the patron saint of Spain, Mary herself had facilitated the defeat of indigenous Mexica warriors. Records indicate that they believed James and Mary had fought shoulder to shoulder with Spanish troops; occasionally the two saints were said to have cast dirt into the eyes of their enemies.[39] Accounts indicate that Cortés had images of Mary on his battle standards, and chronicles maintain that he also continued the *reconquista* practice of leaving Marian images in indigenous temples. Louise Burkhart reminds us, "Cortés was following the common Spanish practice of turning mosques in conquered Moorish territories into churches by dedicating them to [Mary]."[40]

So from the onset of Spanish occupation of Mexico, the cults of Mary were prominent. Jacques Lafaye accounts for this development of the Marian cults in Mexico as follows:

> The first historic reason [for her subsequent popular appeal] is the widespread cult of Mary among the leaders of the conquering expeditions, who came from Estremadura or other Iberian provinces. The most famous examples are the brothers Pizarro, natives of Trujillo, and, in the case of Mexico, Hernán Cortés, who came from Medellin. The first Christian images given to the Indians were Saint James, who

appeared to them as a formidable god of war and of thunder, and the Virgin Mary, whose appearance, by contrast, must have consoled the vanquished. The introduction of the Marian cult into the Indies was soon reinforced by the arrival of the first missionaries, especially the Franciscan religious, who were especially devoted to the Virgin Mary.[41]

The arrival of the Franciscan religious came shortly after the fall of the Mexica capital, Tenochtitlán. In 1523, three Flemish Franciscans arrived in New Spain and began to instruct the defeated Mexica in Christianity. The following year, "the Twelve" Franciscans arrived in Veracruz and made a slow procession inland to Tenochtitlán, only to be welcomed with great deference by Hernán Cortés and other prominent conquistadors.[42] The conquistadors, to the amazement of the Mexica, greeted the mendicants by kneeling before them, kissing their hands and the hems of their robes.[43] With this demonstrative display, the "spiritual conquest" of Mexico had begun.[44]

Another traditional depiction of the spiritual conquest of Mexico included the now-popular narrative of the apparition of the Virgin of Guadalupe. Approximately ten years after the coming of the Spanish invaders to the Americas, a miraculous event reportedly took place just north of Mexico City on a hill called Tepeyac. On an early December morning, the Virgin Mary first appeared to a lowly Mexica man named Cuauhtlatozin (Juan Diego) and greeted him in a familiar and loving manner. Her message was one of compassion for the plight of the native inhabitants of Mexico. She instructed Juan Diego to tell the bishop of Mexico at that time, Juan de Zumárraga, a Spanish religious, of her appearance and her desire that a church be built upon the site so that she might be worshiped there. Bishop Zumárraga skeptically received the message, and Juan Diego dejectedly returned to the hill where Mary made a second appearance to report the negative encounter with the bishop. The following day, Juan Diego returned to the bishop, again telling him his account of the apparition, only to be met with skepticism once more. This time, the bishop asked Juan Diego for a sign from Mary as proof of his claims. He returns to Tepeyac where Mary appears again and asks Juan Diego to return to the hill the following day, so that she might provide the sign. Upon returning to his home, Juan Diego was greeted with the news that his uncle had been taken gravely ill. Juan Diego set out to find medical help, which took him all night and most of the following day, so that he neglected Mary's desire that he return for the sign. On the next day, thinking that his uncle's illness would inevitably lead to death, he attempted to find a priest to perform the last rites. To seek a priest, however, he was forced to pass the very hill where he had encountered Mary on the previous days. He took an alternative route around the hill but was discovered by Mary. Mary asked him to ascend the hill, where he found a lovely bouquet of Castillian roses, quite out of season among the indigenous flora. He assembled the flowers in his cloak (*tilma*) and returned to the bishop's residence, where he miraculously displayed the flowers and the imprint of the Holy Mother on his garment. Upon seeing this miraculous event, both men fell to their knees and worshiped.

The implications of this traditional account are that the cult's beginnings are the result of a miraculous appearance of the Virgin to a Mexica peasant. Therefore, popular contemporary accounts frame this as an indigenously based worship. The Spaniard—in this case, the bishop and Franciscan mendicant, Zumárraga—is depicted as a faithless, sign-seeking skeptic. Unfortunately, most of the historical evidence from sixteenth-century Mexico paints a completely different picture of the events that led to the rise of Marian/Guadalupan devotion. In fact, most of the historical evidence from that period points to a strictly Spanish devotion to Guadalupe. Even more remarkable is that, in the following century, indigenous devotion is still minimal; the primary devotees were the Creole population of New Spain.

Evidence for these assertions is not difficult to come by. It is striking that the will of Bishop Zumárrga makes absolutely no mention of either his experience with Juan Diego and the Virgin or of the *ermita* (hermitage) he supposedly founded. This silence about the apparition is consistent with the rest of his writings. How could it be that a man who had experienced what Juan de Zumárraga had supposedly experienced in 1531 could remain silent in his writings, especially in his will, in which, as the *ermita's* theoretical founder, he should have bequeathed it some portion of his possessions? Could it be, as Stafford Poole and others have concluded, that the earliest devotees of the Virgin of Guadalupe in New

Spain were the Spaniards themselves and not the indigenous?[45] Writings concerning the Virgin of Guadalupe in the sixteenth century consistently make no mention of the apparition accounts.

We do have evidence that the Spanish devotion to Guadalupe was seen as a problematic influence on native catechumens. As early as September 9, 1556, Francisco de Bustamante, the Franciscan provincial in New Spain, delivered a sermon in which he explicitly challenged the Mexica appropriation of Guadalupe. He claimed that indigenous devotions to Guadalupe were misappropriations of the Spanish devotion because the Mexica believed the image worked unsubstantiated miracles, that they presented a teaching contrary to what the mendicant orders were teaching them, and that the devotion lacked any theological basis. He proclaimed that if the Mexica devotions continued in their current form, he would stop teaching the natives and that the validity of the supposed miracles must be scrutinized. In his opinion, the penalty for the propagation of the indigenous devotions would be a severe whipping at the hands of a religious inquisitor. Finally, and most fascinating for this current study, is his assertion that the painting of Guadalupe had been created by a native artist.

Bustamante was responding to a sermon that Bishop Montúfar had delivered the previous day (September 8, 1556). According to Poole, Montúfar's sermon can be reconstructed as follows:

> He apparently praised the devotion to the Virgin Guadalupe and made favorable mention of miracles that had been reported at the shrine. He attempted to link the devotion to the Mexican Guadalupe to other major Marian devotions in both Europe and New Spain, such as Remedios, and thus put it in the mainstream of Catholic devotional life. He claimed that the Indians had *no* devotion to the Virgin Mary.[46]

What is most revealing about these two antagonistic religious leader is their perception of how the Mexica were affected by these devotions. For Bustamante, the Spanish devotions were "infecting" and undermining the mendicants' teachings to the Mexica. He even goes on to argue that because the painting is a production of a native artist, its veneration is all the more disorienting for the indigenous. Montúfar, on the other hand, attributes the miracles to Spanish devotions and claims that the "Indians" paid no homage at all. Most striking in these accounts is that in both cases, there is no mention of the traditional apparition accounts.

In 1573 a British corsair named Miles Philips, who was stranded in Mexico after a failed expedition, passed through Tepeyac and visited the shrine. He recorded this visit when he returned to Britain:

> The next morning we departed from thence on our journey towards Mexico, and so traveled until we came within two leagues of it, where there was built by the Spaniards a very fair Church, called Our Lady's Church, in which there is an image of our Lady in silver and gilt, being as high and as large as a tall woman, in which Church, and before this image, there are as many lamps of silver as there be days in the year, which upon high days all are lighted. Whensoever any Spaniards pass by this Church, although they be on horse back, they will alight, and come into the church, and kneel before the image, and pray to our Lady to defend them from all evil, so that whether he be a horseman or a footman, he will not pass by, but first go into the Church, and pray as aforesaid, which if they do not, they think and believe that they shall never prosper; which image they call in the Spanish tongue, Nuestra Senora de Guadalupe.[47]

It is significant in this report that the corsair, like Montúfar before him, portrays a completely Spanish devotion at the *ermita* of Our Lady of Guadalupe in 1573. And, like Montúfar and Bustamante, he makes absolutely no mention of any apparition in connection with the shrine.

In 1576, Bernardino de Sahagún wrote the following condemnation of Guadalupan devotion at Tepeyac:

> Near the mountains there are three or four places where they used to offer very solemn sacrifices, and they would come to them from very distant lands. One of these is here in Mexico [City], where there is a hill called Tepeyacac and the Spaniards call Tepeaquilla and is now called Our Lady of Guadalupe. In this place they used to have a temple dedicated to the mother

of the gods, whom they called Tonantzin, which means our mother. . . . Now that the church of Our Lady of Guadalupe has been built there, they also call her [or it] Tonantzin. . . . The devotion itself is suspect because everywhere there are many churches to Our Lady and they do not go to them. They come from distant lands to this Tonantzin, as they did in former times.[48]

Sahagún, like Bustamante before him, expresses his deep concern for indigenous misunderstandings of what the shrine should represent.

What is clear to the majority of scholars of this period is that, in the sixteenth century, the main devotees of the shrine are the Spaniards. Their deep devotion is what the religious leaders see as a problematic example for the neophyte indigenous Catholics. This conclusion is solidified by the complete absence of any mention of the apparitions by one of the primary actors in the apparition story, Bishop Juan de Zumárraga. Moreover, the accounts of Antonio Freire and Juan de Velasco agree that the *ermita* was not built during the time of Zumárraga, as the traditional account suggests, but rather in the mid-1550s under the direction of Archbishop Montúfar.

It therefore seems clear that the cult of the Virgin of Guadalupe in New Spain was primarily a Spanish devotion in the first century after the conquest of Mexico. There probably was some indigenous devotion, but it was peripheral and closely monitored by the mendicant religious, who were on the alert for pagan undertones. Finally, in the examples just mentioned and in the encyclopedic collection of testimonies collected by Stafford Poole, there is no mention of the traditional apparition accounts prior to 1648. Louise Burkhart reaches this supporting conclusion:

The shrine's principal clientele was the Spanish population of the Mexico City area, who by the early 1600s were attributing miraculous cures and rescues to the devotion. Some Nahuas of the immediate area participated, as evidenced by the 1588 will of Doña Catalina de Siena of Coyoacan, who left four *tomin*, equaling a half peso, to the Tepeyacac shrine. It was not until after the foundation legend was published in Spanish in 1648 and in Nahuatl the following year, that native people outside the Valley of Mexico participated to any significant degree, and even then it was in response to propagation of the cult by Creole priests rather than any particular attraction they felt toward the devotion. In outlying areas, Guadalupe had little impact at the village level before the 1750s.[49]

ANTAGONISM BETWEEN SPANIARDS AND CREOLES, 1521–1648

As years passed after the arrival of the Spaniards in New Spain in 1521, a new class of people emerged in society: the Creoles. Creoles were Spaniards, but they were born in New Spain. Although in theory the Creoles were granted the same legal rights as those who had been born in Spain, in practice the latter considered them inferior. This posture was sometimes

> blamed on geography (they were born too close to the sun) or climate (which made them lazy). Hence a sense of inferiority, not always subtle, was part of the criollo inheritance. Thus, for example, all higher offices in New Spain were monopolized by peninsulars [Spaniards born in Spain]. Of the 171 bishops and archbishops in New Spain in the colonial period, only a handful were criollos. A similar situation prevailed in civil government.[50]

As a result, the presence and growth of the emerging class of Creoles initiated tension with European-born Spaniards. The problem was not so much biological as it was political. These sons and daughters of the Americas instigated and shared a new worldview—one of new beginnings, new opportunities, and new possibilities. In the minds of these first Creoles, the term *New Spain* suggested a break with "old" Spain. So infectious was this new spirit that even some Spaniards were converted to their worldview. Jacques Lafaye contends, "The 'Creole spirit' preceded the birth of the first true Creole; consequently we see 'creolized' Spaniards, come from the peninsula."[51] He continues, "It was knowledge of the country and, above all, loyalty to the colonial ethic of Creole society, rather than the place of birth, that defined the *criollo*."[52]

Again, although framed in biological terms, the real resentment of the Spaniards stemmed from the possibility of this new category of people breaking loyalties with the crown of Spain—a break that had major economic implications for all involved.

This tension was felt acutely within the mendicant orders as well. Spanish religious became increasingly weary of the growing numbers of Creoles in their ranks. The rivalry grew so intense among the Franciscans that "each side attempted to swamp the other by recruiting members from their own group."[53] This rivalry intensified, especially when mendicant provincials were to be selected. Ultimately, a compromise was reached in the selection process. Both groups agreed to a selection system called the *ternas*, whereby Creole and peninsular provincials would be chosen alternately within their respective orders. Within the selection system itself, a distinction was made between Spaniards ordained on the peninsula and Spaniards ordained in the Americas. Therefore, the *ternas* were divided into three major categories: Spaniards ordained in Spain, Spaniards ordained in the Americas, and Creoles.

Not surprisingly, this rivalry influenced Marian devotion in the Americas. Significantly, the Creoles abandoned the first Marian images that came to the Americas. As mentioned earlier in this chapter, the two main Marian images that were imported to the Americas from Spain were the Virgin of Guadalupe and the Virgin of Remedios. The Spaniards remained loyal to these traditions, but toward the end of the sixteenth and throughout the seventeenth centuries, they came to emphasize Remedios. This devotion was no doubt emphasized by the Spaniards because of Remedios's close association with the conquest. According to tradition, a statuette of Remedios accompanied Cortés, carried by one of his soldiers.[54] The statuette accompanied Cortés in the earliest battles with the Mexica, and was purportedly left by Cortés in the great Temple of Huitzilopochtli in Tenochtitlán. It was lost during the night of the *noche triste* (Sorrowful Night), when Spanish troops were driven out of Tenochtitlán by the Mexica, and it was later rediscovered among the shrubbery by an Indian cacique (a native chief in Latin America during colonial and postcolonial times) and an ally of the Spaniards.[55] The cacique took it to his home, where it resided for ten years. It then disappeared, only to be rediscovered at the site where it had first been found. The statuette was returned to the home of the cacique but was miraculously returned to the original site once more.[56]

The Spaniards' emphasis of devotion to our Lady of Remedios toward the end of the sixteenth and throughout the seventeenth centuries is of great importance. This can be directly linked to the rise in Guadalupan devotion on the part of the problematic Creoles, as well as the mestizos (individuals of mixed Spanish and indigenous ethnicity) and other indigenous persons. It was a conscious decision by the Spaniards to separate themselves from the rising ranks of the Creoles.

The Creoles, too, consciously decided to separate themselves from their Spanish counterparts with respect to Marian devotion. Among their ranks, devotion to Remedios was limited at best. Unlike the Spaniards' devotion, their emerging devotional emphasis would be on Guadalupe—but not the traditional Estremaduran Guadalupe. Rather, it would be the Guadalupe of a new creation and a new people, the Creoles of Mexico. It was therefore imperative to distance their Guadalupan devotion from that of the Spaniards. Lafaye speculates on this matter:

> Why did the Indians, or the *Creoles*, their religious guides, feel so clearly the need to distinguish their Guadalupe from that of Estremadura? The question is important, for the event correlates with a birth of tradition of "apparitions" whose raison d'être was the same desire to establish a distance vis-à-vis Spain, as well as the desire to be geographically closer to the site of miracles, thereby relieving pilgrims from having to make the "great voyage" to a distant sanctuary. . . . The change of images was the first step of a Mexican national consciousness.[57]

This change reflects unique differences between the images of veneration in Estremadura and Tepeyac. The Estremaduran version is a dark-colored statuette of Mary adorned in ornate robes. She holds the infant Jesus in one arm and a scepter in the other. The Virgin of Tepeyac is a painting: she does not hold the infant Jesus but may very well be pregnant.[58] Thus, the Virgin of Estremadura and the Virgin of Tepeyac are strikingly dissimilar in appearance.

Even more important are the apparition traditions that arose in the mid-seventeenth century. These traditions helped forge a Creole identity that was distinct from that of the Spaniards. Stafford Poole comments on this emergence of a sense of Creole identity that coincided with the rise of the Mexican Guadalupan apparition accounts:

> In 1648 and 1649 the silence that shrouded the apparitions changed dramatically with the first accounts of them. These were the work of two criollo priests, Miguel Sánchez and Luis Laso de la Vega, who together opened up an abrupt new chapter in the history of Our Lady of Guadalupe. Sánchez, in particular, was responsible not just for first making the story known but also for bonding it to criollo identity.
>
> The appearance of the apparition story coincided with the flowering of criollismo. By the early seventeenth century, the growing number of criollos made them a force to be reckoned with. That and the failure of the dismal prophecies about their eventual physical and mental deterioration meant that they could no longer be disregarded. Though peninsular-criollo antagonisms still existed and broke out into open hostility, the snobbery and the prejudice of the previous century generally assumed subtler forms. The criollos had come to dominate the ranks of the diocesan clergy, for the diocesan priesthood was more open to them than other avenues of social mobility, and the peninsular bishops, who needed the diocesans in their conflicts with the orders, were generally favorable to them. The Jesuits, whose educational work was primarily among the criollos, also tended to be sympathetic.
>
> The eagerness and rapidity with which the criollos, especially the clergy, embraced the new devotion and used it as the basis for a myth of uniqueness and distinct identity show that criollismo had reached a critical mass by the mid-seventeenth century. It needed only the opportunity to express itself, and that opportunity was provided in a special way by Miguel Sánchez. New Spain was not just the homeland of the criollos, it was also the new homeland of the

Virgin Mary, who, through the miracle of her image, had her second birth there. Though initially centered in Mexico City, the new devotion quickly spread outward. For half a century, the image/apparition devotion, which logically should have appealed to the Indians, was exclusively criollo. The fusion of Guadalupe and Mexican identity began not in Tepeyac in 1531 but in Mexico City in 1648. In the story of the apparition criollismo found its legitimacy.[59]

It is with the rise of these Creole apparition accounts that we are able to witness the subversion of Spanish forms of Guadalupan worship. The Creoles, forging a niche for themselves in the New World amid the intense rivalry with their Spaniard counterparts, chose a familiar myth to recontextualize their claims of a unique genesis of a people in a new land. Their agenda was not to only create a myth of origins for their rising sense of criollismo, but to also subvert Spanish claims to superiority in the Americas by attacking their foundational myths. Tracing the Marian devotional loyalties in the Americas establishes the intensifying rupture between these two groups. As the Creoles devised ways to forge a new myth of origins based on familiar patterns of Spanish religiosity, peninsular Spaniards emphasized the manifestation of Mary that related their history with her to the conquest. The battle lines had been drawn, and Creole identity in the Americas would never be the same again.

MIGUEL SÁNCHEZ: ADVOCATE FOR CREOLES

Miguel Sánchez was born in Mexico City in 1594. As a young adult, he studied at the Royal and Pontifical University in Mexico City, where he earned the *licenciado* degree (roughly the equivalent of the contemporary master's degree). He trained as a diocesan priest and was a well-respected educator and preacher as well as an authority on the writings of Augustine. On several occasions, he unsuccessfully attempted to join the faculty at the university. He served as chaplain to the nuns of San Jerónimo and the Hospital Real. In 1662, when he joined the Oratory (the union of the diocesan clergy), he was chaplain of the sanctuary of Our Lady of Remedios. Subsequently, at an undetermined date, Sánchez retired to the *ermita* of Our Lady of Guadalupe, where he lived a quiet life of prayer and poverty until his death in 1674.[60]

His known writings include a Marian novena published in 1665 for use in prayer at the sanctuaries of Guadalupe and Remedios. Most important for this study, however, is his *Imagen de la Virgen Maria, Madre de Dios de Guadalupe, Milagrosamente aparecida en la ciudad de Mexico: Celebrada en su historia con la preofecia del capitulo doce del Apocalipsis* (Image of the Virgin Mary, Mother of God of Guadalupe, [who] miraculously appeared in the City of Mexico: Celebrated in her history, with the prophecy of chapter twelve of the Apocalypse), published in Spanish in 1648. His writing style has been described as "baroque, meandering and highly metaphorical,"[61] and he has been condemned for his lack of historical documentation, praise of pious tradition, and overt Creole nationalism.[62]

Sánchez's *Imagen de la Virgen Maria* has been accepted by most Guadalupan scholars as the first published account of the encounter between Juan Diego and Guadalupe to which a date can be attached with certainty (1648). The book begins with approval of the censors, Juan de Poblete and Pedro de Rozas. The censors' approval is followed by a brief introduction by Sánchez, an introductory exegesis of Revelation 12, and an extensive verse-by-verse exegesis of Revelation 12 as a counterpoint to the narration of the apparition of the Mexican Virgin of Guadalupe. Sánchez then describes the procession of December 26, 1531, when the image supposedly was transferred from the cathedral of Mexico City to the ermita. This is followed by a description of the ermita and a set of related miracle stories associated with the image.[63]

What is most striking about Sánchez's account is that he wrote it at all. This literary production strongly suggests that he believed the traditional Estremaduran Guadalupe myth required an Americanized counterpart, just as the Estremaduran icon required an Americanized icon. This Americanized Guadalupan myth marks a departure from any traditional loyalties that Sánchez or his Creole brothers may have had toward the Estremaduran Guadalupe. Even more striking in this departure is that he maintains the topographic reference in her name, Guadalupe, thus enhancing the echoes or allusions to the Iberian Guadalupe. He directly adapts the Iberian form of the myth while simultaneously recreating or, as I will argue in this chapter, subverting it. Miguel Sánchez, a Creole caught in the crosshairs of a long-running rivalry between Spaniards and Creoles, locates himself in an exegetical tradition of subverting the very myths used to justify one people's domination and control of the "others." He is challenging the empire by subverting the empire's very own ideological apparatus.

How does Sánchez accomplish this with his *Imagen*? Again, I emphasize that the mere act of creating an Americanized form of the myth to coincide with the Americanized icon is an act of ideological departure. Sánchez also emphasizes the Creole claim of New Spain's divine election. This is accomplished by finding a correlation between Tepeyac and the Garden of Eden and also by his emphasis on the similarities between the Queen of Heaven in Revelation 12, with her importance in the birth of Christianity, and the hierophany of Guadalupe and the birth of the church in the New World.[64] On this matter, Lafaye suggests that Sánchez is "the true founder of the Mexican *patria*":

> For on the exegetic bases which he constructed in the mid-17th century that *patria* would flower until she won her political independence under the banner of Guadalupe. From the day that Mexicans began to consider themselves a chosen people, they were potentially liberated from Spanish tutelage.[65]

Sánchez himself asserts that he was motivated to write this account on behalf of "the homeland, my people, companions, citizens, those of this *new world*."[66] He acknowledges that the Creoles had an "intimate and special brotherhood of relationship with Mary in this her image, since she is reborn miraculously in the land where they are born."[67] He asserts that the image of Guadalupe is "the first Creole woman, a native of this land."[68] He goes on to make a backhanded attack on the Spanish notion that Creoles were somehow inferior, based on their exposure to the extreme climate of the Americas, by asserting that Mary herself had advocated for them against the elements: "Most holy Mary took control of the sun, moderated its rigors, reduced its heat, calmed its fire, tempered its rays, served as a cloud."[69]

Sánchez's exegetical logic anticipated many of the claims Spaniards had made concerning the supposed inferiority of the Creoles. Along with the special election of the Creoles in the Americas, Sánchez created what amounts to a mandate that subverts previously constructed social hierarchies as maintained by the Spaniards. Even more significantly, Sánchez wrote his account at a moment in the history of the Americas when the numbers of Creoles, in contrast to Spaniards, was reaching a critical point. Spaniard migrations to the Americas could not keep up with the reproduction rates of the Creole population. This was also reflected in various political and religious positions that Creoles were coming to dominate by virtue of their numbers. According to Poole,

> Criollismo is the central theme of [Sánchez's] book … the story
> of the apparitions is little more than a framework on which
> Sánchez can build his criollo interpretations. … It is impossible
> to trace the subsequent history of the Guadalupe devotion
> without the awareness that it was a criollo devotion, in which
> the sons of the land saw their own special election.[70]

Twelve years after the publication of Sánchez's *Imagen*, a Jesuit named Mateo de la Cruz published anonymously "an abbreviated and vastly improved account of Sanchez's work."[71] This publication was very popular and was perhaps as vital in the spread of Guadalupan devotion as the original. It simplified the sometimes convoluted language of Sánchez and focused on the apparitions themselves without the complicated exegesis of Revelation 12. It is the first account to give the now-accepted dates for the apparition, December 9–12. Another interesting feature of this text is that de la Cruz omits Sánchez's overt criollismo. He does, however, note the increasing rivalry between Our Lady of Guadalupe and Our Lady of Remedios, which reflects the continuing problems between the Spaniards and the Creoles. Perhaps for the first time in print, de la Cruz also names Guadalupe as La Criolla, and Remedios as La Conquistadora.[72]

It is only appropriate that I should cite counterarguments or, more precisely, counterconcerns of authors on why someone like Miguel Sánchez would appropriate and subvert the Spanish Guadalupan myth. I have argued that he did so in order to undermine Spanish claims to power and the Spaniards' air of superiority to the Creoles in general. Others have reservations about this thesis. Timothy Matovina quite correctly notes that in the *Imagen*, Sánchez proclaims Mary as the Spanish assistant conqueror. Matovina also argues that Sánchez asserts that the criolla Guadalupe

> complements the Spanish Our Lady of Remedios in a manner that parallels the biblical figures of Naomi and Ruth. Like Naomi, the native of Bethlehem, Guadalupe was a native of Mexico; like Ruth, Remedios was a foreigner who migrated to provide her love and assistance in a new land. Both virgins are equally deserving of veneration. References such as these reveal that, though the seeds of *criollo* nationalism planted in Sánchez's text would soon bear fruit among his fellow American-born priests and their compatriots, reading *Imagen de la Virgen María* as a patriotic oration expressed in theological language by no means exhausts the meaning of this crucial work in the development of the Guadalupe tradition.[73]

Jacques Lafaye, in support of Matovina's conclusion, argues, "To make Miguel Sánchez a premature Mexican revolutionary would be an anachronism." Yet he continues, "But he certainly was a Creole patriot, fully conscious of being one."[74]

My response to these two cautions is best made with a nuance of their argument. In my concluding chapter, I will argue that resistance is most commonly accomplished with subtle acts of subversion, rather than outright rebellion or revolution. From a logistical perspective, subtle forms of resistance make more sense, since those who are "other" are generally not in the position to engage the "center" in outright defiance. Miguel Sánchez, as Matovina has suggested, planted that all-powerful ideological seed by subverting the very myth used to de-center him and other Creoles of the Americas. This, indeed, gives us a clue as to why Sánchez appropriated the text of Revelation 12 in his work. Revelation 12, like the countermythology of Sánchez in the *Imagen*, sought to undermine not the structures of oppression but the ideologies that stood behind those structures.

Therefore, the cautions of Matovina and Lafaye should be taken seriously. Sánchez was not a true revolutionary compared with the likes of Miguel Hidalgo y Costilla, who with his *grito de Dolores* (shout of

Dolores) would overtly mobilize Mexicans against the Spanish occupiers two centuries later. Rather, Sánchez dealt in a more subtle and perduring form of resistance—ideological resistance. He mastered, in the words of James Scott, the art of "hidden transcript."[75]

Another interesting aspect of Sánchez's *Imagen* is the battle he wages against any indigenous claims to the apparition tradition. Most Guadalupan scholars deny the existence of any such tradition, but all feel compelled to comment about it. For example, Robert Choquette, Charles H. Lippy, and Stafford Poole state, "In all probability it was a legend that grew up amongst the Indians in the late sixteenth or more probably early seventeenth century to explain the origin of the shrine and to bring comfort to an oppressed people."[76] Louise Burkhart exclaims, "Where the legend really came from, including the extent to which the indigenous people may have participated in its formulation, remains unknown."[77] Matovina alludes to the possibility of an existing tradition that Sánchez may have used as his point of departure: "Did the reports of Juan Diego's miraculous encounter with Guadalupe initiate the shrine and its devotion, as Sánchez's book claims, or is the apparition narrative a later invention, perhaps of Sánchez himself, that provides a mythical origin for an already existing image and *pious tradition*?"[78] Jean-Pierre Ruiz goes one step further by acknowledging a pre-Sánchez account of Guadalupe: "It is clear that Sánchez sought to advance the *criollo* agenda by means of this work, which recast the *traditional account* of Guadalupe, directed as it was toward the Nahuatl-speaking people of Mexico, and re-directed it on behalf of the Mexican-born descendants of the *conquistadores*."[79]

Ruiz's suggestion of the possibility of a pre-*Imagen* Guadalupan myth is complicated by the fact that the story Sánchez ultimately spins is clothed within the framework of an apparition genre very common in European religious circles. However, this does not imply an absence of a Mexica account that Sánchez ultimately desired to displace with his work. Regardless of whether this proto-Guadalupan myth existed, Sánchez "took a cult story that should have been exclusively Indian and appropriated it for the criollos."[80] This is especially obvious when one compares the text of Luis Laso de la Vega, written just six months after *Imagen*, in which Laso de la Vega emphasizes an indigenous agenda in his Guadalupan myth.[81]

One can conclude, therefore, that if there was a pre-*Imagen* Guadalupan tradition that advocated for the indigenous of the New World, then Sánchez fought a battle on two fronts: one against the Spaniards, the other perhaps against an artistic or oral tradition that viewed Guadalupe as a protagonist in favor of indigenous peoples. In light of Sanchez's own words, this second front may not be such a stretch:

> With determination, eagerness, and diligence I looked for documents and writings that dealt with the holy image and its miracles. I did not find them, although I went through the archives where they could have been kept. I learned that through the accident of time and events those that there were had been lost. I appealed to the providential curiosity of the elderly, in which I found some sufficient for the truth.[82]

Judging from his own words, therefore, it is perhaps safe to assert that an indigenous tradition did exist prior to Sánchez writing his *Imagen*, and that he did have some knowledge of such tradition. This does not, however, detract from the fact that Sánchez produced the first account of the apparition tradition with a Creole agenda opposed to the Old World Guadalupe myth and to any indigenous speculation that indigenous peoples may have had concerning the image and its relative meaning for their population. Sánchez, therefore, in spite of his baroque and convoluted style, produced a manifesto for Creoles as God's chosen people in Mexico against both the natives of Spain and of the Americas. Ultimately and with great finesse, using the technique of mythological subversion, this Creole priest took ownership of a myth that would be foundational for present and future claims of Creole chosenness.

LUIS LASO DE LA VEGA: ADVOCATE FOR THE INDIGENOUS OF MEXICO

Within six months of the original publication of Miguel Sánchez's *Imagen*, a second treatise was published in 1649 by Luis Laso de la Vega, vicar of the *ermita* at Guadalupe.[83] Little is known about the life of Laso de la Vega, except that he received the position of *medio racionero*[84] in 1657 and that he was one of two contributors of laudatory letters for

Sanchez's *Imagen*. The title of his work is *Huei tlamahuiçoltica omonexiti in ilhuicac tlatocacihuapilli Santa Maria totlaçonantzin Guadalupe in nican Huei altepenahuac Mexico itocayocan Tepeyacac* (By a great miracle the Heavenly Queen, Saint Mary, our precious Mother of Guadalupe, appeared here near the great Altepetl of Mexico, in a place called Tepeyacac). No other publications by Laso de la Vega are known to exist. Interestingly, his work is written not in Spanish, as is Sánchez's *Imagen*, but in Nahuatl, the native tongue of the Mexica. The *Huei tlamahuiçoltica* was given church approval by the Jesuit censor Baltasar Gonzáles.[85]

The text can be divided into six separate sections: (1) a personal introduction by Laso de la Vega; (2) the apparition accounts, also known as the *Nican mopohua*; (3) a description of the painting; (4) a list of the miracles performed at the *ermita* known as the *Nican motecpana*; (5) a description of the life of Juan Diego; and (6) a final exhortation and prayer.[86]

The primary relevance of Laso de la Vega's work is that he was well aware of Sánchez's *Imagen*. Although he contributed a laudatory letter for the work, he felt compelled to write his own version of the apparition stories just six months later.[87] The question, therefore, is whether Laso de la Vega's work is consistent with Sánchez's or whether it is possible to identify differences between them, which would raise the question of Laso de la Vega's agenda in writing this second account.

First, I note that Laso de la Vega wrote his account in Nahuatl, the native tongue of the Mexica. Sánchez, who wrote his treatise in Spanish, no doubt targeted the Creoles of the Americas as his projected audience, as discussed in the previous section. I agree with Barbara Harlow that "The very choice in language in which to compose is itself a political statement on the part of the writer."[88] Is it therefore fair to conclude that Laso de la Vega targeted the indigenous peoples of Mexico with the *Huei tlamahuiçoltica*? This may well be the case, but we must also ask what other groups would have had the ability to read Nahuatl in the mid-seventeenth century in the Americas. Perhaps the only other group with such an ability would have been the Spanish clerics who missionized and educated the indigenous peoples: "It had the Nahuas (and perhaps the ecclesiastics conversant with Nahuatl) as its intended readership."[89] What is most fascinating about the attempt to identify Laso de la Vega's target

audience is that the indigenous demonstrate no evidence for a substantial
devotion to Guadalupe prior to the eighteenth century. This does not
mean, however, that Laso de la Vega did not target this group, only that
his efforts to evangelize them were *initially* unsuccessful.[90]

The second possible target audience, the Spanish clerics whose Creole
numbers were swelling in the mid-seventeenth century, is an intriguing
alternative. If Laso de la Vega was responding to the work of Sánchez—
whom we know for certain was targeting Creole audiences—what was
the message Laso de la Vega was attempting to convey? A brief analysis
of the *Huei tlamahuiçoltica* reveals some interesting possibilities. The
introduction of the work states its main intention:

> That is what moved and encouraged me to write in the
> Nahuatl language the very great miracle by which you have
> appeared to your people and have given them your image
> which is here in your precious home in Tepeyacac. May the
> humble commoners see here and find out in their language
> all the charitable acts you have performed on their behalf,
> [the memory of which] and their circumstances had been
> lost according to the nature of time's passage.[91]

Laso de la Vega asserts that he wrote in order that the Mexica might
come to better (re)acquaint themselves with the apparition tradition of
Guadalupe in which the Mother of God herself has performed miraculous
charitable acts on their behalf. In light of Sánchez's *Imagen*, this is an
interesting departure from Sánchez's overt *criollismo*. Although it would
be inaccurate to state that Sánchez has no indigenous agenda, it is fair
to say that this agenda is downplayed in his text in favor of his Creole
spin. Therefore, speculation that Sánchez borrowed from a preexisting
indigenous tradition becomes much more tenable. To state, as most
commentators do, that Sánchez downplayed the indigenous aspects is
to recognize a previous oral and/or written tradition. This argument is
supported by the claim that Laso de la Vega also employed a previous
apparition account: "[It appears] that the indigenous aspect was central
and original, that Laso de la Vega's version owes its ascendancy."[92]
Nevertheless, the relevant point is that Laso de la Vega "indigenizes" the
Creole tradition—of which we are sure he was aware—as maintained in

the *Imagen*.[93] Also, it is quite clear that Laso de la Vega wrote his treatise with the intention of downplaying the Creole sensibility of the *Imagen* in favor of an indigenous sensibility. On this matter, most commentators are in agreement. Poole notes that "Laso de la Vega's few commentaries tended to stress the Virgin Mary's love and compassion for the Indians." He continues, "Unlike Sánchez, Laso de la Vega did not identify the Virgin of Guadalupe with criollismo; rather, he pictured her as the mother and protectress of the Indians, toward whom she shows special love."[94] According to Jean-Pierre Ruiz, "The [*Huei tlamahuiçoltica*] appealed to its intended audience by tapping traditional Nahua religious symbolism. The [*Imagen*] wrapped the Mexican Guadalupe in the mantle of the New Testament canon that was familiar to the *conquistadors* and their children,"[95] whether they had been born in Spain or the Americas.

It is therefore possible that Laso de la Vega was attempting to initiate indigenous worship of Guadalupe by massaging the story with indigenous language and symbolism while simultaneously appropriating and subverting the Creole ideology behind Sánchez's *Imagen*. In an apparent move to downplay the Creole flavor of the apparition accounts, Laso de la Vega advocates for a group that he believes needed a compassionate and caring message. Again, as Sánchez subverted the traditional Spanish account as it was employed during the *reconquista* and conquest of the Americas, so too, Laso de la Vega employs a myth of a dominant group (the Creoles) and turns it on its head.

Just as Sánchez fought a two-pronged battle (contra Spaniards and the Mexica), so too it can be argued that Laso de la Vega's myth is multivalent. Laso de la Vega also takes the opportunity in his text to address the Spanish devotion to Our Lady of Remedios, the preferred devotion of Spaniards in the eighteenth century. Recall that an apparition tradition also emerged from a statuette of Remedios that was left in the central temple of Huitzilopochtli by Cortés. For the Spaniards, she became much more closely associated with the conquest after the development of a Guadalupan cult by their rivals, the Creoles.

In the conclusion to the *Huei tlamahuiçoltica*, Laso de la Vega provides an interesting comparison between Guadalupe and Remedios. In his description of the history of the latter, he states, "For her precious image came along with the Spaniards when they first entered and came to

make war."[96] He goes on to discuss the subsequent disappearances of the
image and its miraculous reappearances. He even goes on to describe the
miracles that were ascribed to the image. Therefore, to the casual reader
of Laso de la Vega's conclusion, the first appearance of his account leaves
the impression of his acceptance of and gratitude for Remedios. However,
he goes on to describe Guadalupe by contrasting the *miraculous* origins
of the icon:

> Especially she about whom we are speaking set up her
> residence here at Tepeyacac and by a great miracle gave
> people her image, which no earthly human artist made or
> colored. It was she herself who made her own copy, because
> she lovingly saw fit to make her residence there.[97]

What strikes the reader when comparing these two descriptions is that
(1) Guadalupe is described as uniquely American in contrast to Remedios,
who is a Spanish import; and (2) Remedios is a man-made statuette, albeit
with the capacity to perform miracles, whereas Guadalupe is presented as
an icon not made by human hands. Although the contrast is only implicit,
it is nevertheless quite striking. Poole stresses, "More so than Sánchez,
Laso de la Vega sought to subordinate Remedios (which later became the
Spanish devotion) to Guadalupe (the criollo and Indian devotion)."[98] Even
more striking is that when Laso de la Vega describes another set of "man-
made" icons, those of the indigenous of the New World, he asserts thus:

> For in that time there was no lack of respected people and
> precious friars who had long been servants of the heavenly
> Queen, and she did not grant any of them the favor of
> revealing herself to him, but only to the humble commoners
> who were submerged in the night of darkness, and even
> though the faith had already reached their ears, they were
> still cherishing and serving the false little gods that were only
> hand-made images of our enemy the demon.[99]

Here, Laso de la Vega overtly attacks indigenous idolatry, but he also
appears to be simultaneously attacking Spanish devotion on two fronts.
The first and most obvious is that the Virgin of Guadalupe chose not
to appear to devout Spanish religious but rather to humble commoners.

The second is his polemic against hand-made images. Thus resulted the comparison of the three sets of images:

> Remedios: human-made and imported
> Guadalupe: heaven-made and domestic
> Indigenous idols: human-made and domestic

Is it possible that Laso de la Vega has set up this comparison to counter any claims of iconographic superiority made by the Spaniards or the indigenous? And is it possible, with his emphases on heaven-made versus human-made, that Laso de la Vega is covertly attacking Remedios as being, at the very least, theologically suspect? We may never know the answer to these questions, but it is evident, as Poole concludes, that Remedios is being subordinated to Guadalupe in these passages. Therefore, both Sánchez's Imagen and Laso de la Vega's *Huei tlamahuiçoltica* subordinate Remedios to Guadalupe.

CONCLUSION

In the Americas, the Creoles and the Mexica shared a social and cultural reality, namely, the explicit and implicit domination of their peoples by the conquistadors from Old World Spain. As a result of this marginalization, both groups—as an act of both offensive and defensive resistance—subverted an "imperial" myth that created the social hierarchy favoring the Spaniards. The lens that would focus and shape this recontextualization of the Spanish Guadalupan myth was Revelation 12, a text deeply embedded in its own imperial entanglements, thereby establishing a genealogical relationship between first-century Asia Minor and seventeenth-century Mexico. Sánchez proposed "that the woman clothed with the sun of Revelation 12 corresponds to Our Lady of Guadalupe, and that [Revelation 12] furnishes the key to understanding the apparitions and the image, and their significance for Mexico."[100] In his rendering of the myth, he reorders power, transferring the benevolence of Mary from the invading Spaniards to the marginalized Creoles, in much the same way as early Christians shifted the emphasis from the offspring of Leto, Apollo, to the offspring of Mary, Jesus. It is a classic case of how people living on the margins of power ideologically challenge centers of power.

The same case can also be made for the work of Laso de la Vega. As his laudatory letter regarding Sánchez's work shows, Laso de la Vega was well aware of the work of his contemporary but decided almost immediately to write his own recontextualized version of the Guadalupan myth from the context of the indigenous people of Mexico. He too subverted the "imperial" myths (Spanish and Creole) to advocate for the humble commoner of the land. Both Sánchez and Laso de la Vega represent the marginalized, writing with a critical eye toward the center, but Laso de la Vega writes from a position considerably further from that center.

CHAPTER 3

SUBVERTING MILLENNIAL MYTHS TODAY: MANIFEST DESTINY AND *EL PLAN ESPIRITUAL DE AZTLÁN*

MANIFEST DESTINY: MYTHOLOGICAL JUSTIFICATION FOR WESTWARD EXPANSION AND SUPPRESSION OF INDIGENOUS PEOPLES

THE CHICANA/O MOVEMENT (see pp. 94–101 below) is not monolithic, and, therefore, since the middle of the twentieth century, it has subverted and challenged several aspects of U.S. ideology. Close examination of Chicana/o rhetoric of the late 1960s and early 1970s, however, reveals one ideological tradition that the movement challenged specifically: "Manifest Destiny." This is especially true of the treatise *El Plan Espiritual de Aztlán* (The Spiritual Plan of Aztlán).[1] In this chapter, I therefore begin by examining how the ideology of Manifest Destiny facilitated U.S. claims to Mexican territories, and then describe the subsequent Chicana/o polemical rhetoric that explicitly challenges this ideology.

Richard T. Hughes, in *Myths Americans Live By*, makes the following observation about how Americans tend to describe themselves:

> Among the most powerful and persistent of all the myths that Americans invoke about themselves is the myth that America is a chosen nation and that all of its citizens constitute a chosen people. Scholars and statesmen often refer to this myth as the myth of American exceptionalism. The label

"American exceptionalism," however, obscures the profoundly religious origins of the chosenness vision. It is one
thing to claim that America is exceptional in its own eyes. It is
something else to claim that America is exceptional because
God chose America and its people for a special mission in
the world.[2]

At the very core of Hughes's analysis is the notion that national (that
is, imperial) myths are employed to say something about a people and
how that people sees itself in relation to the rest of the world.

Figure 1. American Progress, by John Gast (1872)

This myth of exceptionalism is especially obvious in artistic
representations of the nineteenth century. One such example, John Gast's
painting *American Progress* (1872), portrays Euro-American settlers
being led to western territories by Lady Providence/Columbia (see
Figure 1). Note that she leads not only settlers but progress in the form of
telegraph wires (which she herself is laying), railroad tracks, trains, ships,
bridges, and weaponry. Fleeing her/their advancement are the beastly and

cowardly hordes portrayed by the indigenous of the land and by animals associated with the West. This artistic expression makes exceptional claims about the Euro-American subject in contrast to the indigenous object, the "other." As a result, the claim of national exceptionalism, especially an exceptionalism based on the mandates of God, represents a proclamation of both spiritual and national superiority. This self-understanding lies at the heart of nineteenth-century conceptions of Manifest Destiny.

In 1845, when a New York journalist named Louis O'Sullivan coined the term *Manifest Destiny*, he was describing a situation that already was "writ large on the hearts and minds of the American people long before the term itself appeared in print."[3] After the War of 1812, indigenous lands west of the Appalachians were made "available" for Euro-American expansion, thereby initiating a period of tremendous migration. Between the years 1810 and 1820, the Euro-American population west of the Appalachians doubled.[4] In the mid-1800s, incursions into Texas and the Oregon territories contributed to the ever-increasing spirit of American expansionism. In an editorial in the journal *Democratic Review*, O'Sullivan justified the annexation of Texas by creating a term that would represent this emerging civic faith: a presumed right

> of our *manifest destiny* to over spread and to possess the whole of the continent which Providence has given us for the development of the great experiment of liberty and federative development of self-government entrusted to us. It is [a] right such as that of a tree to the space of the air and the earth suitable for full expansion of its principles and destiny of growth.[54]

The most striking quality of this declaration is how embedded it is in the religious language of exceptionalism and its direct allusion to Providence. O'Sullivan's words made explicit a feeling, which had begun to develop in earnest after the Revolutionary War, that the United States was being guided by the hand of God and had been given a "God-sanctioned mission to fulfill."[6] According to Robert Johannsen,

> fundamental to the feelings of national superiority generated by romantic nationalism was the conviction that American

territorial expansion was inevitable, that the nation's providential destiny—its Manifest Destiny—decreed an extension of the ideals of its founding charter throughout the entire continent. The notion was all the more credible because American settlers, traders, and missionaries were already on the move to far distant areas of North America.[7]

This emerging sense of national destiny was neither a liberal nor a conservative endeavor but rather "cut across partisan and sectional lines; Whigs as well as Democrats, Southerners as well as Northerners expressed it."[8] Frederick Merk, a well respected historian of U.S. history, also sheds light on the deep rooted sensibilities in nineteenth-century expansionist movements. In his description of the general intentions behind Manifest Destiny advocated by many nineteenth-century U.S. citizens he notes:

> It [Manifest Destiny] was less acquisitive, more an opportunity for neighboring peoples to reach self-realization. It meant opportunity to gain admission to the American Union. Any neighboring peoples, established in self-government by compact or by successful revolution, would be permitted to apply. If properly qualified, they would be admitted.[9]

Merk continues his analysis and includes an important citation from O'Sullivan's article on Manifest Destiny which makes specific reference to Mexico: "Some—the Mexican, for example—might have to undergo some schooling for a time in the meaning and the methods of freedom before they were let in."[10]

The ideology of Manifest Destiny is not without its critics in the American academy. Biblical scholar Burton Mack in his monograph *A Myth of Innocence* has convincingly argued that the Christian gospel continues to be the lens through which Western culture has viewed the world. For Mack, however, this relationship between Western culture and the Christian gospel is a volatile alliance:

> In America, especially, popular culture and Christian mythology have intertwined to produce a strong secular sense of destiny. The combination of new land, new people,

and the challenge of constructing a new society along egalitarian lines seemed to justify the sense of fulfilling a divine mandate.[11]

For Mack, embedding the Christian gospel in notions of U.S. exceptionalism created an unstable and dangerous combination of innocence and power that resulted in the justification of violence to convert one's enemies: "American presence is held to be good for the other country, a sign of expansion of the American way of life. Largesse rejected thus creates dismay. Then it is that thoughts turn ugly, to the use of force to save the world from its demons."[12]

Mack recognizes that the ideology of Manifest Destiny, when spun as an "opportunity" for the underdeveloped, can lead to devastating consequences for those who reject the advance. In those cases where conversion fails, annihilation is the next and natural option. With this ideology as background, Euro-American occupants of the United States believed that

> there is a sense that something fundamental is wrong with the world, something that must be destroyed or transformed to assure the peaceable kingdom. . . . Unwilling to join the human race, to settle for less than the kingdom of God, an apocalyptic mentality is again in evidence.[13]

The workings of the U.S. notion of Manifest Destiny touched many people and events. The specific example that I will consider in this chapter involves the War with Mexico (1846–1848).

THE U.S.–MEXICAN WAR OF 1846–1848 AND THE TREATY OF GUADALUPE HIDALGO

The migration of Euro-Americans into the vast territories of Texas, then under the sovereignty of Mexico, was well under way by the mid-nineteenth century. In 1844, after the election of President James Polk, a major proponent of the annexation of Mexico, war between the United States and Mexico appeared inevitable. In fact, Polk interpreted his electoral victory as "a mandate of national expansion."[14] But even before Polk took over the presidency, President Tyler called on Congress to annex Texas, and in the final days of his presidency (December 1845), Texas became a state.

The main point of contention for Mexico was not that the United States had annexed a part of its vast northern territories (Mexico had long recognized that it could not control or monitor the vast number of Euro-American immigrants moving into Texas), but rather that the United States acted in poor faith by claiming the territorial boundary to be the Rio Grande rather than the traditional line of demarcation, the Nueces River. As a result of this disagreement, Polk stationed U.S. troops in the disputed area, impeding any diplomatic solution to the standoff. In March of that year, reports arrived in Washington, D.C., that Mexican troops had fired on the troops of General Zachary Taylor in the disputed territories. Upon hearing the reports from Texas, Polk drafted a declaration of war against Mexico, and on May 13, 1846, Congress formalized the declaration.

What were the intentions of President Polk and the U.S. public at the time? Was this simply a U.S. president looking out for a part of his constituency in disputed territories, or was Polk being an opportunistic land-grabber, like many of the Euro-American immigrants already in Texas? According to historians Ray Billington and James Hedges, many in the United States convinced themselves of a more noble intention:

> Every patriot who clamored for Mexico's provinces would indignantly deny the desire to exploit a neighbor's territory. The righteous but ill-informed people of that day sincerely believed their democratic institutions were of such magnificent perfection that no boundaries could contain them. Surely a benevolent Creator did not intend such blessings for a few; expansion was a divinely ordered means of extending enlightenment to despot-ridden masses in near-by countries. This was not imperialism, but enforced salvation. So the average American reasoned in the 1840's when the spirit of manifest destiny was in the air.[15]

Once again, U.S. intentions for expansion into western territories were shrouded in the innocent cloak of Manifest Destiny. The power of this myth to justify American expansionism cannot be overstated. Rodolfo

Acuña asserts, "Land was the primary motive for the war."[16] To this Albert Weinberg adds, "The enlargement of territorial aim was probably due less to philanthropy than to a consideration of national self-interest."[17] Indeed.

Another relevant component of the ideology of Manifest Destiny is the dehumanization of those who do not willfully participate in this "great" democratic experiment. This is especially true in the case of the U.S.–Mexican War. James McCaffrey comments on how U.S. troops regarded their Mexican enemy:

> They regarded all human beings with darker skins as being on a lower level of human evolution than themselves. Many gave evidence of this in their frequent comparisons of Mexican peasants with Indians of the American West and black slaves of the American South. The debasement of the Mexicans served a military purpose in that the troops had less difficulty in taking the lives of enemy soldiers [and enemy noncombatants] if they considered them to be subhuman.[18]

The general rhetoric of the day spoke of an explicit attempt to regenerate the degenerate and unfortunate Mexican peoples. An article in the *U.S. Democratic Review* stated, "Mexico is in a state of suspended animation. She is in fact dead. She must have resurrection. She must be electrified—restored."[19] Walt Whitman argued that the Mexican race must be thoroughly chastised.[20] It is not difficult to discern the implicit cultural and racial notions of superiority embedded in the U.S. ideology of Manifest Destiny and its violent ramifications.

Accounts from the war attest to atrocities unleashed by American forces. The doctrine of "convert or destroy" was taken to unfathomable extremes. One American eyewitness, George Meade, described the situation in Monterrey, Mexico, on December 2, 1846: "They [American forces] plunder the poor inhabitants of everything they can lay their hands on, and shoot them when they remonstrate."[21] On July 9, 1846, he made the following observations concerning U.S. volunteer forces:

> They have killed five or six innocent people walking in the street, for no other object than their own amusement. . . .

They rob and steal the cattle and corn of the poor farmers, and in fact act more like a body of hostile Indians than civilized Whites. Their officers have no command or control over them.[22]

Various memoirs also record the actions of American troops during the occupation of Mexico. Samuel Chamberlain, a soldier, recorded the following scene in a journal entry concerning the volunteer forces during the conflict in the Mexican city of Parras:

On reaching the place we found a "greaser" shot and scalped, but still breathing; the poor fellow held in his hands a Rosary and a medal of the "*Virgin of Guadalupe*," only his feeble motions kept the fierce harpies from falling on him while yet alive. . . . Soon shouts and curses, cries of women and children reached our ears, coming apparently from a cave at the end of the ravine. Climbing over the rocks we reached the entrance, and as soon as we could see in the comparative darkness a horrid sight was before us. The cave was full of our volunteers yelling like fiends, while on the rocky floor lay over twenty Mexicans, dead and dying in pools of blood. Women and children were clinging to the knees of the *murderers* shrieking for mercy. . . . Most of the butchered Mexicans had been scalped.[23]

These are just a few examples of how U.S. enlisted and volunteer forces conducted themselves during their occupation of Mexico. Dehumanization of the "other" justified maltreatment and atrocities during times of war. Cloaked in the mythology of Manifest Destiny, the dehumanization of Mexican people was the inevitable result of the understanding perpetuated by a national sentiment that recognized the mandate of its citizenry as having a divine mission to spread U.S. culture, democracy, and ideologies to the underdeveloped masses. From the perspective of the United States, this was not imperialism but "*enforced* salvation."

In the end, the Mexican army and citizenry were ill prepared for this formidable incursion into their northern territories. When General

Scott landed on the coast of Veracruz and marched more than 12,000 troops to the extremities of Mexico City, the outcome of the war had been forcefully decided. On May 19, 1848, with the signing of the Treaty of Guadalupe Hidalgo, hostilities officially ended between the two nations.

Several historians and commentators have taken the philanthropic ideals of Manifest Destiny to task with respect to the U.S.–Mexican War. Peter Michel argues that Polk had decided to invade Mexico far prior to any "assault" by Mexican troops on General Zachary Taylor and his forces in the disputed regions of Texas. Acuña, summarizing Michel's argument, lists the following prewar goals of Polk as they relate to seizing Mexican territories:

> Polk planned the campaign in three stages: (1) Mexicans would be cleared out of Texas; (2) the United States would occupy California and New Mexico; and (3) U.S. forces would march to Mexico City to force the beaten government to make peace on Polk's terms.[24]

Although most U.S. historians have argued that Mexico was at fault for initiating the war, Michel's assertions do not appear to be off base, especially when one considers that Polk believed his electoral victory was a mandate for continued national expansion. In the mid-1840s, the only realistic area for expansion was the sparsely populated lands to the west that were part of Mexico. As a result of the war, the boundary between Mexico and the United States was set at the Rio Grande and Gila River. Along with Texas, the United States also acquired the Mexican territories of Arizona, California, Nevada, New Mexico, western Colorado, and Utah. The total land seizure was estimated at approximately 1,360,000 square kilometers (525,099 square miles) and expanded the United States' territorial claims to the Pacific Ocean. In return, Mexico received $15 million.

The Treaty of Guadalupe Hidalgo was ratified by the Mexican and U.S. governments, resulting in the eventual armistice between the warring nations.[25] However, this treaty was prepared and altered amid some controversy. In the treaty, Articles VIII, IX, and X were developed specifically with concern for Mexicans living in their traditional lands now under the governance of the United States. Articles XIII and IX guaranteed former Mexican nationals now living in the United States the full rights of U.S. citizenship, as well as the additional benefits of maintaining their capacity to practice their native customs, laws, and religion. Article X, the locus of the majority of the controversy, was initially written to protect prior land and property titles. In essence, Article X protected all property and land claims of Mexican citizens developed under the Mexican government and transferred such claims under the new governance of the United States with the expectation of full recognition.

The controversy began when the U.S. Senate deleted Article X from the treaty. The Mexican government protested, and the U.S. Senate responded on May 26, 1848, *not* by reinstating Article X, but rather by developing a "Statement of Protocol." The protocol read as follows:

> The American government by suppressing the Xth article of the Treaty of Guadalupe Hidalgo did not in any way intend to annul the grants of lands made by Mexico in the ceded territories. These grants . . . preserve the legal value which they may possess, and the grantees may cause their legitimate (titles) to be acknowledged before the American tribunals.
>
> Conformable to the law of the United States, legitimate titles to every description of property, personal and real, existing in the ceded territories, are those which were legitimate titles under the Mexican law of California and New Mexico up to the 13th of May, 1846, and in Texas up on the 2nd of March 1836.[26]

The reconfigured Treaty of Guadalupe Hidalgo was ratified by the narrowest of margins by the Mexican Congress in the summer of 1848.

Unfortunately, from a Mexican landowner's perspective, the U.S. government took full advantage of the ambiguous language in the protocol ("These grants . . . preserve the legal value *which they may possess*") to act in bad faith. Ultimately, the ambiguous language left Mexican land claims to the mercy of the U.S. courts.[27] In retrospect, Chicano activist Armando Rendón contends that

> the omission of Article X resulted in the [U.S.] federal
> government seizing millions of acres of land from the states,
> affecting the descendants of Mexicans and Native Americans
> left behind. Based on this sleight of hand, in New Mexico
> alone, the federal government seized 1.7 million acres of
> communal land.[28]

As a result of the ideology of Manifest Destiny, of the U.S.–Mexican War, and of the broken Treaty of Guadalupe Hidalgo, a devastating legacy of race relations between the former combatants became the norm, and that legacy remains to this day. With the influx of Mexican migrants into the United States in this post-9/11 era, the ugly head of U.S. notions of exceptionalism has reared itself once again. However, now with full territorial claims to lands once owned by Mexico, philanthropic intentions have long since dissipated. The once-open gates of the "temple of freedom" have long since been closed. Rhetoric of increased border patrols, "citizen patrols," and comprehensive border boundaries flourish. Xenophobia is in fashion once again, leading to the dehumanization and stereotyping of the most vulnerable of peoples. Voices call for violence in order to control the invading hordes.

Although the war and the treaty were nineteenth-century events, in the 1960s and '70s, a new generation of Mexican Americans would revisit this moment in history and would "redefine their position within the United States using in part, the Treaty of Guadalupe Hidalgo. They called themselves Chicanas/os."[29] I now turn to this subversive moment in history, a moment that would appropriate and subvert the American ideology of Manifest Destiny, the ideology at the very core of American justifications for the war with Mexico and the Treaty of Guadalupe Hidalgo.

THE CHICANA/O MOVEMENT

During the late 1960s and early 1970s, a new political consciousness emerged among socially conscious Mexican-American youths in the southwestern United States. The designation *Chicana/o* signifies a departure from both the dominant Euro-American society and those Mexicans and Mexican-Americans who maintained Spanish and/or Anglo self-understandings. I therefore use the term to focus on one form of ethnopolitical resistance that was adopted by the movement at a specific period in our history.

According to Rudy Acuña, the preeminent voice in Chicana/o studies in the United States today, the term *Chicana/o* is at best a "contentious" label.[30] He describes the multivalence of the term as follows:

> To some it includes only Mexicans born in the United States, while for others it encompasses those born on either side of the border. The arrival of large numbers of Central Americans has generated a third school, which accepts this new reality by using *Chicano* as a political term rather than one referring to a single nationality.[31]

Chicana/o originated as derogatory term employed by Anglo landowners in the southwestern United States in the early twentieth century to refer to Mexican farm workers. The native tongue of many of these workers was not Spanish but the indigenous Nahuatl, in which language the word *mexicanos* was pronounced *mesheekanos*. Landowners, therefore, began referring to their Mexican employees as *sheekanos* (Chicanos). Matt S. Meier and Feliciano Rivera, somewhat differently, contend that *Chicana/o* was originally derived from the word *Mexicano*, which through elision was transformed to *Xicano*, the letter *X* in Nahuatl being pronounced as *s/sh*, which resulted in the current spelling, *Chicana/o*.[32] Meier and Rivera also note that the term was used pejoratively by upper-class Mexicans to refer to Mexicans from the lower classes. In any case, the term was originally used as a derogatory label for working-class, indigenous Mexicans in both the United States and Mexico.

In 1969, at the First National Chicano Youth Liberation Conference, held in Denver, disenfranchised Mexican-American students from throughout the Southwest proactively adopted the label *Chicana/o*. Their adoption of the term signified two noteworthy emerging sensibilities. First, Chicana/o activists were well aware of the Black civil rights movement's self-designation *Black* in favor of the externally imposed term *Negro*. They recognized the potential for self-empowerment by claiming a once-derogatory label on their own, redefined terms. This subversion of a once-derogatory term "achieves its significance in being chosen and given political legitimacy by Chicano activists. . . . The appropriation of this word marked the exceptional sense of power which naming oneself signifies."[33] It was one of the first steps in Chicana/o self-determination.

The second emerging ideology reflected by this adaptation was the active decision of Chicana/o activists to politicize the movement. The decision to adopt the label *Chicana/o* within the context of an emerging Chicana/o political identity "signifie[d] an identification with struggles for change within or the transformation of socioeconomic and political systems that have historically exploited Mexicans and people of Mexican ancestry."[34] Acuña accentuates this point by noting that this now-political term "embraced [the] collective responsibility to bring about social change for their community and their country."[35] Chicana/o self-labeling was an act of empowerment that deconstructed and resignified a once-derogatory term, allowing it to be used politically. I use *Chicana/o* here primarily as a term of ethnopolitical resistance that was adopted by the movement in its earliest expression.

The war between Mexico and the United States left a bitter legacy of hatred and suspicion. A major aspect of this negative legacy was the stereotypes about Mexicans embedded in the sensibilities of many U.S. citizens. Américo Paredes's work *With His Pistol in His Hand: A Border Ballad and Its Hero* summarizes these stereotypes, which he convincingly shows were in evidence among the Texas Rangers, the U.S. Border Patrol, and also in the mid-twentieth century with U.S. servicemen who were engaged in a series of attacks (riots) with Mexican and *Chicano* "Zoot Suiters" in Los Angeles:

1. The Mexican is cruel by nature. The Texan must in self-defense treat the Mexican cruelly since that is the only treatment the Mexican understands.

2. The Mexican is cowardly and treacherous. . . . He can get the better of the Texan only by stabbing him in the back or by ganging up on him with a crowd of accomplices.

3. Thievery is second nature to the Mexican. . . . On the whole he is about as degenerate a specimen of humanity as may be found anywhere.

4. The degeneracy of the Mexican is due to his mixed blood.…
   He is descended from the Spaniard, a second-rate type
   of European, and from the equally substandard Indian of
   Mexico.[36]

The negative legacy of these stereotypes is evident in Chicana/o polemics of the 1960s and '70s. Regarding conditions in the rural areas, Chicanas/os targeted the substandard wages of the farm workers, the lack of education for their children (many of whom, because of low-paying jobs, were forced to work alongside their parents), illiteracy, harsh labor conditions, exposure to poisonous chemicals, and the vicious cycle of abject poverty. Some of the most acute and significant urban issues were police brutality, civil-rights violations, land proprietorship, inadequate housing and social services, and being taught that their cultural heritage and language served as a hindrance to their success (English only!). For most Chicanas/os living in the United States during the 1960s and '70s, these realities were reflected in a 25 percent high school graduation rate, an unemployment rate double the national average, and income levels for Chicanas/os that were about two-thirds of what their white U.S. counterparts earned for the same work. The Vietnam War also was a major issue for Chicanas/os, for they made up a disproportionate amount of U.S. casualties in Southeast Asia, and their contributions were not valued.[37]

As a result of these dehumanizing civil-rights violations and following the example of the Black civil-rights movement under the direction of Rev. Dr. Martin Luther King Jr. and others, the Chicana/o movement became explicitly political:

> The Chicano political movement grew out of an alliance
> in the 1960's of farmworkers struggling to unionize in
> California and Texas, the disenfranchised and dispossessed
> land grant owners of New Mexico, the urban working classes
> of the Southwest and the Midwest, and the growing student
> movement across the country. All of these were essential
> participants in the Chicano Movement.[38]

At the very genesis of the Chicana/o movement stood César Chávez and the National Farm Workers Association (the precursor to the United Farm Workers union). Although the UFW was not officially part of the movement, its struggles were the impetus for the ever-growing political consciousness of young Chicanas/os in the southwestern United States. Even more important, the UFW and Chávez brought national and worldwide exposure to the civil-rights demands of Chicanas/os in the United States. This exposure is best attributed to the support of presidential candidate Robert F. Kennedy and fellow civil-rights activist Martin Luther King Jr. Chávez also generated much attention to the plight of Mexican and Chicana/o farm workers with his well-publicized hunger strike of 1968. Later in 1968, Chávez, along with thousands of supporters, marched from the heart of California farm country to the steps of the state capitol in Sacramento.

The rallying cry of the marchers and the farm workers movement in general was "*Justicia para los campesinos y viva la Virgen de Guadalupe!*" (Justice for the farm workers and viva the Virgin of Guadalupe).[39] The Virgin of Guadalupe's banner was flown at the front of the caravan and carried by many of the marchers.

The symbolism of Guadalupe stood at the heart of and as the impetus for the subsequent Chicana/o movement. Yet, the use of her image was multivalent from the very beginning. Chávez, a devout Catholic, no doubt employed Guadalupe to demonstrate that his movement was embedded in Catholic doctrines of social justice and was not at all related to the various Marxist movements in Latin America of that day. Commentators such as Goldman and Ybarra-Frausto emphasize this point.[40] Are there any other reasons why Chávez and the UFW would use Guadalupe as one of two basic symbols for the farm workers movement (the other being the red, black, and white Aztec eagle, which would become the main secular symbol of the movement)? Is it possible that Chávez—like Miguel Hidalgo y Costilla, arguably the founder of modern-day Mexico—employed the Virgin in a much more politically subversive way?

Miguel Hidalgo y Costilla, a Creole priest and theologian, on the morning of September 16, 1810, rang the church bells in the Mexican city of Dolores and exclaimed the transcendent *grito de Dolores* (shout of Dolores) of the revolution against Spanish occupation: "Death to the

Spaniards! Long live the Virgin of Guadalupe!" With this cry and the support of thousands of Mexican peasants, Hidalgo began the struggle to expel Spain from Mexico after almost three hundred years of occupation. It was in its purest form an example of overt postcolonial revolution. On these matters, Hidalgo was drawing on the writings of sixteenth- and seventeenth-century Jesuits who were ultimately expelled from Mexico by the Spanish crown and who wrote extensively on the tyrannical nature of Spanish domination.[41]

I do not contend that Chávez would have been schooled in early Jesuit writings but rather that he was well aware of the subversive manner in which a variety of Mexican and Chicana/o social revolutionaries had employed Guadalupe in the past. Not only was she used subversively, but subversively in matters of *control of the land*. Chávez was not so idealistic as to attempt to reclaim the lands lost by Mexicans after the U.S.–Mexican War (although later Chicana/o activists would do so); he simply employed Guadalupe's iconography to argue for humane conditions in which to work the land. In most commentaries regarding Chávez's use of the Virgin, however, there is a myopic focus on the religious implications and a neglect of the sociopolitical implications.

The sociopolitical implications that Chávez and the UFW had anticipated came to full expression in the work of the Federal Alliance of Land Grants (FALG) under the leadership of Reies López Tijerina. With this movement and the subsequent development of *El Plan Espiritual de Aztlán* at the First National Chicano Youth National Conference in Denver in 1969, we see explicitly demonstrated the movement's subversion of U.S notions of Manifest Destiny.

The main contention of Tijerina and the FALG was that for centuries the United States had stood in violation of the Treaty of Guadalupe Hidalgo, which ended the U.S.–Mexican War of 1846–1848. It was therefore the main goal of the FALG to acquaint peoples of Mexican descent of their rights in reference to historic claims to Spanish land grants covered by the Treaty of Guadalupe Hidalgo.[42] Tijerina sought to challenge all U.S. land claims made after the Spanish land grants prior to the early nineteenth century. He argued forcefully that the United States had stood in violation of Articles VIII and IX (recall that Article X had been omitted from the final draft), which specifically "guaranteed property and citizen rights to

Mexicans."[43] Although Tijerina never saw the fulfillment of his dream of having these lands returned to their native claimants, he too set the groundwork for a flourishing nationalistic ideology among Chicana/o intellectuals and activists. According to Griswold del Castillo,

> the Treaty of Guadalupe Hidalgo and its implications became a topic of discussion at the First Annual Youth Conference in Denver, Colorado, which was organized by [Corky] Gonzalez in 1969. Knowledge of treaty violations became a driving force behind the final statement of the conference in "El Plan Espiritual de Aztlan," a document of Chicano solidarity and a declaration of independence. . . . The Treaty of Guadalupe Hidalgo became a focal point for claims of social and economic justice during the activist 1960s and 1970s through militant action, popular books, and scholarly studies. An important legacy of the Chicano movement is its fostering of a particular historical awareness: the Southwest is really "occupied Mexico," and Mexican Americans and Indians are "colonized people" whose rights have been violated despite the guarantees of the treaty.[44]

Before dealing with the specifics of *El Plan*, it is compelling to note the combined force of such emerging ideologies. In 1972, Chicano activist Armando Rendon published his *Chicano Manifesto*, in which he argued, "The Treaty of Guadalupe Hidalgo is the most important document concerning Mexican Americans that exists."[45] He argued convincingly that the spirit of the treaty had been violated by the United States, and he challenged Chicanas/os, as Tijerina had done half a decade earlier, to become aware of the "exact processes by which the Treaty of Guadalupe Hidalgo was made meaningless over the last century and a half."[46]

Commenting on the *Manifesto*, Griswold del Castillo argues that Rendon "had in mind a detailed commentary case that could be made against the [U.S.] federal government so that some kind of compensation could be exacted. He hinted that Chicanas/os could seek, as American Indian tribes had, monetary settlements or even a *return of territory* to Mexico."[47]

Also in 1972, the Brown Berets (a Chicana/o nationalist activist group active during the Chicana/o Movement) began a twenty-four-day occupation of Santa Catalina Island off the southern coast of California.[48] Again, according to Griswold del Castillo,

> a particular interpretation of the meaning of the treaty of Guadalupe Hidalgo influenced the Brown Berets' decision to stage a symbolic occupation of Santa Catalina Island. None of the nine Channel Islands off the coast of Southern California had been mentioned in the treaty as part of the territory ceded to the United States in 1848. . . . The Brown Berets did not seriously believe that they could regain Catalina for Mexico. The real purpose of the occupation was to provide a forum for discussion of the problems confronting Mexican Americans arising from their colonized status. . . . The Santa Catalina occupation demonstrated the degree to which some were willing to take militant action based on the historical violations of the Treaty of Guadalupe Hidalgo.[49]

Whether interpreted literally or metaphorically, the writings and movements that were spawned by such leaders as Reies Lopez Tijerina and Armando Rendon were challenging historic claims to former Mexican territories now under U.S. control based on (re)interpretations of the Treaty of Guadalupe Hidalgo. The treaty, not an ideology in itself, was rather the product of American expansionist ideologies fueled by the religiopolitical concept of Manifest Destiny. As I will argue in the next section, *El Plan Espiritual de Aztlán* has embedded within its corpus explicit language that challenges the ideology of Manifest Destiny and continues the tradition begun by Miguel Hidalgo y Costilla and perpetuated by César Chávez, Reies Lopez Tijerina, Armando Rendon, the Brown Berets, and numerous other Chicanas/os of the 1960s and early 1970s. And just as Hidalgo y Costilla and Chávez had conjured the multivalent (re)significations of the beloved Virgin de Guadalupe in their defense, so too would the emerging Chicana/o Movement.

EL PLAN ESPIRITUAL DE AZTLÁN (THE SPIRITUAL PLAN OF AZTLÁN)

Over the Palm Sunday weekend of 1969 (March 27–31), Rodolfo "Corky" Gonzales—a professional boxer and leader of the Denver chapter of the Crusade for Justice—organized the First National Chicano Youth Liberation Conference in Denver, Colorado. According to Armando Navarro, "The cardinal purpose of the conference was to provide direction and cohesion to a Movimiento that was becoming disjoined and fragmented, and at the regional level needed direction. At best it was a potpourri of numerous local and area youth groups and leaders that lacked a cohesive network."[50] The conference was attended by some two thousand Chicana/o activists and has long been considered the "most important conference held during the epoch of [Chicana/o] protests."[51] The final product of the conference was the drafting of the controversial *El Plan Espiritual de Aztlán*, which was inspired by the intellectual musings of Chicano writer and poet Alberto Ulrista (Alurista). The plan had a multifaceted agenda:

> In the early period, the youth and students of the movement developed a cultural nationalist philosophy that was separatist in nature. The utopian "El plan spiritual de Aztlán" (The Spiritual Plan of Aztlán) . . . was the most influential expression of that philosophy. It called for reclamation and control of lands stolen from Mexico (the U.S. Southwest), anti-Europeanism, and insistence on the importance of glory of the brown-skinned Indian heritage, and an emphasis on humanistic and nonmaterialistic culture and education.[52]

The phrase "reclamation and control of lands stolen from Mexico" echoes the ongoing challenge to the Treaty of Guadalupe Hidalgo and the polemic against the expansionist ideology that stands behind it, namely, Manifest Destiny. This trajectory of thought becomes even more evident when one examines the preamble to *El Plan* itself:

> In the spirit of a new people that is conscious not only of its proud historical heritage, but also of the brutal "Gringo" invasion of our territories: We, the Chicano inhabitants and

civilizers of the northern land of Aztlán, from whence came our forefathers, reclaiming the land of their birth and consecrating the determination of our people of the sun, declare our power, our responsibility, *and our inevitable destiny.*

We are free and sovereign to determine those tasks which are justly called for by our house, our land, the sweat of our brows and by our hearts. Aztlán belongs to those who plant the seeds, water the fields, and gather the crops, and not to the foreign Europeans. We do not recognize capricious frontiers on the Bronze Continent.

Brotherhood unites and love for our brothers makes us a people whose time has come and whose struggle against the foreign "Gabacho," who exploits our riches and destroys our culture. With our heart in our hands and our hands in the soil, We [sic] declare the *Independence* of our Mestizo Nation. We are a Bronze People with a Bronze Culture. Before the world, before all of North America, before all of our brothers in the Bronze Continent, We are a Nation, We are a Union of Free Pueblos, We are Aztlán.[53]

What is most striking about the preamble to *El Plan* is the allusion to U.S. Constitutional language, beginning with the ideology of "we the people," as demonstrated in Alurista's repetitive employment of *We* in the upper case. It is also possible to discern in the last paragraph his parallelism to the U.S. Declaration of Independence when he states, "We *declare* the Independence of our Mestizo Nation." These are powerful allusions that appropriate and subvert the very language used by the founders of the United States in their foundational documents.

Most compelling, albeit more subliminal, is Alurista's pronouncement that the Chicana/o reclamation of lost Mexican territories is "*our inevitable destiny.*" Juxtaposed as it is with calls for the reclamation of lands, can this be anything other than a direct reference to and challenge of Manifest Destiny—the ideology that initially fueled American expansionism into Mexican territories—which *El Plan* ultimately attempts to subvert? Given Alurista's penchant for harking back to the very documents that Americans consider foundational, such an intentional echo is probable.

Unfortunately, this connection is never made by Chicana/o studies scholars, who tend to focus on the sociopolitical dimensions of the Chicana/o movement to the neglect of its religiopolitical components. I suggest that Alurista empowered his constituency by redeploying the very myths that he believed were oppressing Chicanas/os—a legitimate strategy for contesting power from the margins. *El Plan Espiritual de Aztlán* is on one level a subversion of the U.S. ideology of Manifest Destiny.

Another important aspect of *El Plan* is the introduction of the concept of Aztlán into the lexicon of the Chicana/o movement. In its most basic sense,

> Aztlán has come to represent a nationalist homeland, the name of that place that will at some future point be the national home of a Chicano people reclaiming their territorial rights. It has also come to represent the land taken by the United States in its nineteenth-century drive to complete its manifest destiny.[54]

Today, for many Chicana/o intellectuals "Aztlán" refers to multiple postcolonial contests. Rafael Pérez-Torres notes that, from its genesis, Aztlán has signified those northern territories from which the Aztecs migrated until their ultimate settlement in the Valley of Mexico. Aztlán also represents the territories that Mexico lost in the U.S.–Mexican War. Finally, Aztlán represents the utopian concept of where a future Chicana/o nation would be built.

The rhetoric of Alurista combines the ideal mythic past with the ideal mythic future but forcefully notes the irruption of nineteenth-century Euro-American expansion into the region. Therefore, it comes as no surprise that one aspect of the Chicana/o movement was the idealization of their Aztec past.[55] This allowed Chicana/o intellectuals to be critical of another moment in their history when European expansion interrupted their history—the Spanish conquest of Mexico and the Aztec nation. The power of juxtaposing these two moments of conquest cannot be overstated and can be compared to the equating of Rome with Babylon in the book of Revelation (for example, Revelation 18).

According to Perez-Torres, a third contestation can be included in the evocation of Aztlán:

> From a historical perspective…three moments of contestation are evoked in the naming of Aztlán: the Spanish invasion of the Aztec Empire, the appropriation of the Mexican lands by the United States in the nineteenth and early twentieth centuries, and the immigration to (or reconquest of) the U.S. Southwest by Mexicanos and Central Americans in the contemporary era.[56]

Perez-Torres insightfully establishes that the concept of Aztlán is a multivalent contestation of power challenging the traditional depictions of two colonial moments, the Spanish conquest of Mexico and the westward expansion of the United States in the eighteenth century and its continuing neocolonial policies. Although I recognize the multivalent nature of both *El Plan* and the concept of Aztlán, I want again to emphasize that, at the drafting of *El Plan*, Alurista and other Chicana/o activists sought to appropriate and subvert the foundational language of the Declaration of Independence, the U.S. Constitution, and the ideology that fueled nineteenth-century U.S. territorial expansion, specifically, Manifest Destiny. And just as the concept of Manifest Destiny portrayed the regions of the U.S. Southwest as a utopian space, so too does the concept of Aztlán as developed in *El Plan*.

In the plan, however, the land is not to be newly discovered and invigorated (an ideology that contributed to the notion of innocent U.S. expansionism) but rather recognized as the land that was lost due to the "brutal Gringo invasion of our territories." The concept of Aztlán as developed in *El Plan* is not framed in an innocent cloak of romantic "expansionism," but rather in the language of reconquest. It is simultaneously a utopian and non-innocent recasting of space. It is a space marked by the large-scale presence of people of Mexican ancestry living there with their beloved and subversive Virgin of Guadalupe. It is a space marked by the presence of the black eagle of the United Farm Workers flag in direct contrast to artistic representations of the U.S. bald eagle. And, arguably, it is a space—according to *El Plan*—that is truly the northern territories of Mexico rather than the southwest of the United States.

ART IN THE CHICANA/O MOVEMENT: MURALISM AND THE VIRGIN OF GUADALUPE

From the very onset of the Chicana/o movement, art played a critical role in portraying the emerging ideological posture of *la raza*.[57] The primary artistic form during this period was the mural (see the appendix). As a result, Chicana/o barrios were transformed into a kaleidoscope of colors and evocative portrayals of an emerging Chicana/o sensibility.

The mural is both a public expression and a performance that draws the viewer into a critical dialogue with it: "To study an art form is to explore a sensibility, that such a sensibility is a collective formation. . . . [Art forms] materialize a way of experiencing, bring a particular cast of mind out into the world of objects, where [people] can look at it."[58] Although Clifford Geertz is here speaking of art in general, his comments are especially true of the mural. To study the mural is indeed to study a sensibility as a collective formation. The murals that were created during the early days of the movement not only were the products of an individual's artistic interpretation of an ideology but also were a collective cultural representation. They were the products of artists in conversation with other artists and with casual observers who would frequently engage the creator on their projects. The mural was public performance, inviting all who would view it to dream and/or challenge the emerging representation of a people. Geertz's acknowledgment that art is an experiential way of bringing about a certain cast of mind holds especially true for the Chicana/o mural of the late 1960s and '70s.

Ybarra-Frausto takes this observation one step further:

> At significant junctures in our human development we ask and respond to fundamental questions concerning our self-identity, our history, and our future. The same questioning occurs within groups of people at particular moments in their historical trajectory. For Mexican-descended people in the United States, the 1960s was such a period of introspection, analysis, and action. . . . [As a result] Chicanos asserted their historical imperative as generators of culture rather than mere receptors of cultural expressions from the dominant culture.[59]

According to Ybarra-Frausto, the Chicana/o murals were descriptive of a critical juncture in the collective Chicana/o psyche in relation to self-identity, history, and future. It was a defensive strategy in that it sought to counter portrayals of Mexicans and Chicanas/os by the dominant culture of the United States, and it was an offensive strategy in that it framed these discourses as a production of our own Chicana/o cultural generation.

The Chicana/o mural was a public challenge to the dominant society and an invitation to and for creative discourse among *la raza*. As such, it provided Chicanas/os with "the symbolic representation of collective beliefs as well as a continuing re-affirmation of the collective sense of self."[60] Therefore, Chicana/o muralism of the late 1960s and early 1970s was truly an art of *resistance*:

> The mural movement resulted from an almost "spontaneous combustion," influenced directly or indirectly by the strikes and boycotts of the United Farm Workers union, the militant Chicano Movement, and the spiritual and cultural concerns of writers and artists who were active in the movement.[61]

Chicana/o muralists derived their original inspiration from a number of predecessors: "from the social art movements of the Mexican muralists, such as Diego Rivera, José Clemente Orozco and David Alfaro Siquieros, who pioneered the rebirth of public art in Latin America."[62] According to Goldman,

> Mexican muralism was originally created to play a social role in the post-revolutionary period of modern Mexico. It was clearly an art of advocacy, and in many cases it was intended to change consciousness and promote political action. . . . Its other role was educative: to convey information about the pre-Columbian heritage. . . . The role of [Mexican muralism] was to restore understanding and pride in the heritage and cultures that the concept of Spanish superiority had subverted.[63]

The very soul of postrevolutionary Mexican muralism is best described as an attempt to represent the ideals of a struggling middle-class and peasant population against the hierarchies of past governmental leadership, the Catholic Church, which supported the deposed government, and foreign investors. Therefore, the Mexican muralists' movement was simultaneously an art of advocacy and an art of sociopolitical resistance. It was these attributes that Chicana/o muralists found most compelling nearly a half century later. The Mexican muralists inspired Chicana/o muralists to create a critical art of advocacy while simultaneously projecting a new collective vision for a people. It was vital for later Chicana/o artists to draw on an artistic model derived from their own culture, namely, the Mexican muralists. They would not and could not draw from the bourgeois modernistic art of European culture because they were immersed in a comprehensive critique of it. As a result, the Mexican muralists were vital to Chicana/o artistic sensibilities in both their form and their critical posture against the perceived center.

The Mexican and Chicana/o muralist movements did, however, have some striking differences, which Cockcroft and Barnet-Sánchez summarize in this way:

> This new [Chicana/o] movement differed in many important ways from the Mexican one. It was not sponsored by a successful revolutionary government, but came out of the struggle of the people themselves against the *status quo*. Instead of well-funded projects in governmental buildings, these new murals were located in the *barrios* and ghettos of the inner cities, where oppressed people lived. [The murals] served as an inspiration for struggle, a way of reclaiming a cultural heritage, or even as means of developing self-pride. Perhaps most significantly, these murals were not the expression of an individual vision. Artists encouraged local residents to join them in discussing their contents, and often, in doing the actual painting. . . . This element of community participation, the placement of murals on exterior walls in the community itself, and the philosophy of community input, the right of a community to decide on what kind of art it wants, characterized the new muralism.[64]

The differences between the two movements underscore some interesting developments in the half century that separated them. The

Mexican murals portrayed a sensibility derived from the working class contra the Mexican and foreign-born ruling elites. There was also a strong anticlerical sentiment in many of the murals, underscoring the perceived relationship between the Catholic Church and the elite classes. The murals, therefore, are best described as representative of the postrevolutionary national cultural renewal movement. They were representative of the changing postrevolutionary realities of the Mexican nation and its people. During this period, according to Desmond Rochfort, "Mexico underwent an enormous transformation from a mostly rural, semi-literate revolutionary nationalist society to a developed, largely industrialized modern country."[65]

Chicana/o muralism, unlike its predecessor, can be categorized as a collective production of the masses. It was the vision of a people and not so much a vision of the ideologues for a people. As such, Chicana/o muralism was much more of a grassroots movement than its Mexican predecessor had been. One difference is that many of the most prominent Mexican muralists were considered masters of the art form and were trained in Europe. In contrast, most of the Chicana/o muralists were less cosmopolitan, having been trained in the barrios of the southwestern United States.

Another prominent difference between the artistic representations of these two periods is the prominent employment of the Virgin of Guadalupe in Chicana/o muralism from the very genesis of the movement. As noted earlier in this chapter, during the organization of the United Farm Workers under César Chávez, "Two strong visual symbols became central to the Chicano visual artists. The Virgin of Guadalupe and the red, black, and white thunderbird flag [of the UFW] appeared in virtually every procession and demonstration."[66]

The ubiquitous and early use of the Virgin of Guadalupe as a symbol of anticolonialism and justice had a tremendous impact on the emerging religiopolitical posture of the movement. When Dolores Huerta, the UFW's coleader, was asked about the importance of Guadalupe for Chávez, she responded that the Virgin was "a symbol of the impossible . . . that with faith you can win. . . . In our strikes we always have the Virgin with us. That's important *palanca* [moral support]."[67] It can therefore be argued that the subversive symbolism of the Virgin was embedded in the collective unconscious of Chicanas/os and Mexicans, including Chávez, especially at critical junctures in our history. The 1960s and 1970s were no doubt one such critical moment for the UFW. Chávez was well aware of the history of Emiliano Zapata's employment of the Virgin in his battle over land rights with the Mexican government in the early twentieth century. Chávez's grandfather fought with Zapata's revolutionary forces, a significant detail in his story.

The use of the Virgin in such art during the period of critical analysis of the Treaty of Guadalupe and Manifest Destiny deserves some parsing. Recall that one of the strongest contentions during the early years of the movement was that the territories of the Southwest were in actuality occupied Mexico, and that such lands—as Aztlán—should be returned to its former inhabitants. This is consistent with two other critical moments in Mexican history. The first is the account of Juan Diego's apparition of the Virgin. Although written by a Creole religious, this account advocates for an indigenous individual whose people had just lost their land to a colonial power.[68] Second, Hidalgo's employment of the Virgin to mark the beginning of the revolution against the still-occupying Spaniards also challenges traditional accounts of land ownership.[69] It might also be argued that the Virgin was used as a countersymbol to feminine representations of the goddess Providence in nineteenth-century American art, as in John Gast's *American Progress* (see figure 1).[70] In contrast to Gast's Providence stands the indigenous Guadalupe, who at least among Chicana/o activists is the primary symbol of a movement seeking to reclaim that territory known as Aztlán (see Figure 2).

Whether or not Chicana/o muralists of the twentieth century were aware of such artistic expressions from the nineteenth century is uncertain. But the phenomenon of artistically codifying myths and countermyths does speak to the power of ideological artistic representations on both sides of the Manifest Destiny equation. It is therefore possible to imagine that in different historical moments, both Providence and Guadalupe serve as critical countersubversions of each other.

Figure 2. Cesár Chavéz speaking at a United Farmworker walkout in the Coachella Valley, California, with a poster of the Virgin of Guadalupe at his side (1972). Copyright © Oscar R. Castillo, Coachelle, 1972.

It is also noteworthy that post-1975 Chicana/o murals reflect a different set of meanings than their earlier counterparts. Murals evolved. Any analysis of such murals must take account of their routinization. Different historical moments draw from unique sociocultural matrices of meaning. In brief, I do not believe that the barrio Virgin of today (see the appendix for representations of second- and third-generation renditions of Guadalupe) conveys the same charismatic meaning that she did some three and a half decades ago. Whereas the early murals focused on the movement and its accompanying ideologies, today's murals have taken on a more international worldview. Themes such as the unity of all marginalized peoples—regardless of cultural heritage—and solidarity with Central American peoples and issues have emerged. Also, muralists themselves have become more ethnically diverse, and each group has created art based on its people's own specific social locations. Finally, murals have become "centrist" and more palatable to the dominant culture. This has been accomplished through the financing of mural projects by mainstream organizations. The most explicit examples of this mainstreaming are the commissioning of various mural projects in Los Angeles to celebrate the city's bicentennial and the 1984 Olympiad.

However, even in this later period, the murals depicting the Virgin still convey a sense of ongoing resistance. For example, there are the ubiquitous portrayals of her image throughout the barrio as *the* national symbol for Mexico rather than the Mexican flag. One can observe in East Los Angeles today the relative absence of Mexican flags in the neighborhoods—unlike New York City, where Puerto Rican and Dominican national flags are omnipresent throughout the five boroughs. I contend that the absence of the Mexican flag in Los Angeles is a defensive move by people of Mexican ancestry because such displays in the southwestern United States can be viewed as offensive by the dominant society and even interpreted as a reclaiming of former Mexican territories. The flags of other Latin American countries are much more palatable for U.S. citizens because they represent presence rather than "reconquest." What the dominant society does not recognize is the "hidden transcript" of the mural of the Virgin, which remains intact even today. The Virgin is the subversive *bandera* (flag) of Mexicans, and her placement in the barrios of East Los Angeles and the rest of the U.S. Southwest implies not only presence but reclamation. The process of "reconquest" that most U.S. citizens fear is already well under way, and its flag is not that of the former occupants, but the banner of the Virgin of Guadalupe.

CONCLUSION

Mexicans and Chicanas/os have been living with the negative legacy of Manifest Destiny and the Treaty of Guadalupe Hidalgo for more than one and a half centuries. This legacy has left an entire people and their progeny in the unenviable position of choosing between full assimilation into the dominant culture (which is never possible from the perspective of the center) or in a perpetual state of otherness based on maintaining cultural loyalties. Some have chosen the former and have doubly marginalized themselves because the process of assimilation is never comprehensive and their own people have labeled them as *tio tacos*.[71] Those who have chosen the perpetual state of otherness have attempted to negotiate that interstitial space between two cultures—the U.S. and Mexican cultures that they straddle—in a more postcolonial manner. The most significant difference between these two groups is that the former have chosen to remain a colonized people, while the latter have truly embraced a postcolonial mentality in their ongoing neocolonial situation.

The most demonstrative manifestation of this postcolonial mentality was the rise of the Chicana/o Movement in the late 1960s. As Shifra Goldman so eloquently observed, the Movement was a "spontaneous combustion" of a variety of issues that Chicanas/os were facing in this volatile moment in U.S. civil-rights history. It was a time to question everything and challenge those who would oppress under the banner of an innocent-appearing U.S. mythological framework of the melting pot. It was a time when the very myths that the United States employed as foundational would be subversively and sometimes subliminally challenged by the Movement's manifestos, such as *El Plan*.

One such myth that came under the scrutiny of Chicana/o activists was the myth of Manifest Destiny and its injurious progeny, the Treaty of Guadalupe Hidalgo. Chicano activists such as Reies López Tijerina and Armando Rendon excavated the unchallenged history of this treaty and sought both to deconstruct its shortcomings and to construct a basis for reversing its primary tenets. Simultaneously, Chicana/o muralists, taking a cue from the United Farm Workers movement, juxtaposed the Virgin of Guadalupe with all of her postcolonial (re)significations to add a religiopolitical dimension to the secular-political strain of the movement. It was a powerful moment in the history of *chicanisma/o* because her symbolism was so profoundly evocative to so many people of Mexican descent in the United States. I contend that the aspiration of the early muralist movement was to conjure up the traditional readings of the

Virgin contra Spain at both the moment of conquest and at the start of the Mexican Revolution (1812–1821) in order to deconstruct and challenge the new colonizer, the neocolonial United States of America. It was the movement's way of criticizing Rome through the lens of Babylon.

CONCLUSION

The three moments analyzed in this book represent periods in history when disparate cultures have come into contact. In all three cases, there have been significant discrepancies in the distribution of power based on predetermined social hierarchies (imperial versus imperialized, colonial versus colonized, neocolonial versus neocolonized). The common element in these three moments is their relationship to the twelfth chapter of the book of Revelation.

I have attempted to account for the dynamics of and the response to such imbalanced relationships and their ideologies. What language can we employ to articulate this clash of cultures beyond their original subjectivities while simultaneously bypassing one-dimensional notions of cultural syncretism? And what theoretical framework can be employed to explain these encounters? Homi Bhabha, a contemporary cultural critic, offers the following suggestions for theorizing and analyzing colonial situations and their subsequent discourses:

> What is theoretically innovative, and politically crucial, is the need to think beyond narratives of originary and initial subjectivities and to focus on those moments or processes that are produced in the articulation of cultural differences. These in-between spaces provide the terrain for elaborating strategies of selfhood—singular or communal—that initiate new signs of identity, and innovative ideas of collaboration, and contestation, in the act of defining the idea of society itself.[1]

The challenge, as laid out by Bhabha, is for the cultural critic to identify and unpack these "in-between" or interstitial spaces, the desired result being the capacity to assess these "new signs" of cultural identity on both sides of the power equation and to facilitate the articulation of the ambivalent arena of simultaneous collaboration and contestation.

Living in the in-between spaces is the foreground of Bhabha's notion of cultural "hybridity":

> The [cultural] hybrid is neither one thing nor the other but somewhere in-between. Given the power relation between the colonizer and the colonized this in-between usually involves the mimicry of the "master" by the "slave." Colonized people absorb the language and culture of their colonizers, combining it with their own and producing their own hybrid form.[2]

From the perspective of the periphery, hybridity reflects those processes in which the colonized absorb the cultural attributes of their colonizers and combine them with their own indigenous cultural attributes to create a new cultural identity, a new cultural distinctiveness. The resultant hybrid agents, therefore, do not occupy a cultural location that completely reflects the colonizers' culture, nor is it recognizable as the originary indigenous cultural subjectivity.[3]

What separates the hybrid from outdated notions of cultural syncretism is that the hybrid relationship is tinged with the ambivalent desire of wanting one thing while simultaneously desiring its opposite—a more textured departure from simplistic notions of cultural blending. This ambivalence describes the colonial situation in which the colonizer and the colonized are simultaneously attracted to and repulsed by each other's presence in the colonial encounter.[4] This relationship is most significantly recognizable in the process that Bhabha labels "mimicry." In the colonial relationship, the colonizer—in an effort to idealize and label the unequal disbursement of power—"desires the colonized subject to 'mimic' the colonizer, by adopting the colonizer's cultural habits, assumptions, institutions and values, [however] the result is never the simple reproduction of those traits."[5] What occurs in the place of simple and expected cultural appropriation is the rather complex phenomenon of cultural *appropriation* and *subversion*:

> The result is a blurred copy of the colonizer that can be quite threatening. This is because mimicry is never far from mockery, since it can appear to parody whatever it mimics. Mimicry therefore locates a crack in the certainty of colonial dominance, and uncertainty in its control of the behavior of the colonized.[6]

This observation is central to my thesis. As argued in the preceding chapters, those who responded to imperial/colonial cultural impositions in first-century Asia Minor, in seventeenth-century Mexico, and in twentieth-century East Los Angeles all made use of the myths of the dominant power to counter claims to power over them. In first-century Asia Minor, it was the Christian mimicry of the Dragon Slayer myth (the Leto-Python-Apollo myth) in Revelation 12. In seventeenth-century Mexico, it was the Creole mimicry of the Spanish Guadalupan myth located in the works of Miguel Sánchez and Luis Laso de la Vega. And in the twentieth-century Chicana/o movement, it was the mimicry of U.S. notions of Manifest Destiny in *El Plan Espiritual de Aztlán*, which also employed the counter-iconography of the Virgin of Guadalupe.

The responses to these perceived oppressive situations did not involve the creation of a completely new antidiscourse but rather the subversion of what was placed before them as normative in the colonial relationship; it was a counterdiscourse. In the ambivalent existence of most marginal cultures, what occurs is the conundrum of idealizing your occupiers while simultaneously being repulsed by them. The act of subversion or *mimicry* is the offensive and defensive posture taken by the periphery against the center. It is defensive in that it conspires at some level to idealize the center, giving the outward appearance of submission. At the same time, it is offensive in that it seeks to subvert the very discourses that are used to support the colonial hegemony. As a result, mimicry—as in the subversion of imperial myths—is, in fact, a conspiracy of misrepresentation in the face of the dominant culture.

According to James Scott, mimicry can be assessed simultaneously as both "hidden and public transcript" when employed by the periphery. It is a "hidden transcript," representing "a critique of power spoken behind the back of the dominant. . . . It is a discourse that cannot be spoken in the face of power."[7] It is an offstage production never spoken in the face of the dominants. On one level, this is the menace of the mimic agent. But the mimic must also be proximate to the oppressor to be a menace. Therefore, the role of mimicry concurrently functions *also* as a public transcript or that (mis)representation that is palatable to the center—that aspect of the mimic which is "almost but not quite the same."[8] The mimic is, at its very core, a double entendre—simultaneously mimic and menace, public and private, the consummate hybrid.

In first-century Asia Minor, the challenge to the center involved the question of who indeed brought the golden age of prosperity and peace—Augustus Caesar or the Christian mimic, Jesus Christ, as framed in Revelation 12. In seventeenth-century Mexico, the tension is between *la conquistadora*, the Spanish version of the Virgin of Guadalupe, and *la criolla*, the Mexican version of the Virgin of Guadalupe. In twentieth-century East Los Angeles, the battle is played out between U.S. notions of Manifest Destiny and the utopian Chicana/o *El Plan Espiritual de Aztlán* with their accompanying iconographical accomplices, Lady Providence and the Virgin of Guadalupe, respectively. Ultimately, each struggle is between competing countermythologies of the center and its periphery: the dominant myth and its mimic. It is "a struggle over how the past and present shall be understood and labeled."[9] This strategy, as Robert Schreiter notes, recognizes that representations of power can and will be appropriated by the ruled but re-*signified* to promote a peripheral or subaltern agenda.[10]

In the colonizer's desire for a "reformed, recognizable Other, as a subject of difference that is almost the same, but not quite . . . [which] appropriates the Other as it visualizes power,"[11] what emerges is a subjective mimic that is both "resemblance and menace."[12] The ambivalent, subjective mimic and the act of mimicry in general have this perduring effect:

> [The mimic and mimicry in general] locate a crack in the certainty of colonial dominance, and uncertainty in its control of the behaviour of the colonized. . . . [It is] always potentially destabilizing to colonial discourse, and locates an area of considerable political and cultural uncertainty in the structure of imperial dominance. . . . Its ambivalence disrupts the clear-

cut authority of colonial domination because it disturbs the simple relationship between colonizer and colonized. . . . [Therefore, it] reveals the limitation in the authority of the colonial discourse, almost as though colonial authority inevitably embodies the seeds of its own destruction.[13]

From the perspective of the periphery, colonial authority does indeed embody the seeds of its own destruction because the center desires to seek, first and foremost, an ambivalent "almost the same, but not quite like" mimic. Ironically, mimicry is introduced into colonial discourse by the center rather than the periphery and is ultimately the victim of its self-imposed mimesis, whose threat "comes not from an overt resistance but from the way in which it continually suggests an identity not quite like the colonizer . . . [which suggests] that the colonial culture is always potentially strategically insurgent."[14]

With this in mind, Bhabha sees mimicry, a subcategory of hybridity, this way:

[It is] the source of resistance against colonial power, however, not least because it challenges the neat distinction between the culture of the master and the culture [of the] slave. The betweeness of the hybrid challenges the categorical boundaries of the colonial discourse and the sharp distinction it draws between self and other. Furthermore, as a "repetition" it undermines the authority and authenticity claimed for the "original."[15]

As a result, when conceptualizing the idea of hybridity and the closely related terms *mimicry* and *ambivalence* in imperial and colonial contexts, one must look beyond the simplistic notions of the mixing of once-separate cultural traditions. Rather, we must recognize this point:

All culture is an arena of struggle, where self is played off against the purportedly "other," and in which the attempts of the dominant culture to close and patrol its hegemonic account are threatened by the return of minority stories and histories, and by strategies of *appropriation* and *revaluation.*[16]

Therefore, the three specific historical moments analyzed must be evaluated as moments on a continuum of resistance in which we recognize "the complexity of the ways in which this is articulated across a series of relations at the level of the social, not only in the culture of origin but also in the dominant culture of the host institution."[17] I hope to have contributed to delimiting the complexity of countermyths as a reaction to dominant colonial structures and discourses.

Within the larger discourse of postcolonial studies, I hope to have contributed to "the study of imposition and domination as well as of opposition and resistance: not only the discourses of imperialism and colonialism but also the counter discourses of anti-imperialism and anti-colonialism."[18] The only nuance I would add is to rename anti-imperialism and anticolonialism as counterimperialism and countercolonialism. This distinction is valuable especially when employing the theoretical framework of cultural hybridity. The periphery's response to the center's claims to power is created from within the dominant discourses of the center via their adaptation and *subversion*. Therefore, the responses are not random critiques of the myths of the center but highly specific responses using the very framework of dominant discourses. There is no comprehensive rejection of the dominant myths but rather a reconceptualization or a *recontextualization* of them. The response, therefore, is a counterresponse, rather than an antiresponse.

I hope also to have contributed to the analyses of "the different phases within imperialism and colonialism, with their resultant subdiscourses: pre-imperialism and precolonialism; imperialism and colonialism; neo-imperialism and neo-colonialism."[19]

I intend the comprehensive scope of this book—its examination of three historical moments separated by twenty centuries—to enable an assessment regarding whether the subversion of imperial myths is indeed a transtemporal and transcultural phenomenon. My plan was fueled first and foremost by Wimbush's observation, noted above, that if "power is really power insofar as it is comprehensive, sedimented, or profoundly, deeply embedded within every aspect of social order, with the purpose of holding all constitutive elements in place, then there must first always be resistance to it."[20]

I conclude that it is indeed the case that in both imperial and colonial contexts—situations in which power is comprehensive, sedimented, and deeply embedded in the social order—one strategy of power negotiation is the subversion of dominant myths. This way of responding to power is aggressive but subtle. It is aggressive in that it "reveals the limitation in the authority of colonial discourse, almost as though colonial authority inevitably embodies the seeds of its own destruction."[21] The center's desire for the cultural mimic is the genesis of the periphery's creation of the mimic as menace. According to Bhabha, this menace "is itself a process of disavowal . . . [that] poses an imminent threat to both normalized knowledge and disciplinary powers."[22] It is subtle in that, by using the framework of the center, being "counter" rather than "anti," the hybridized mimic is less threatening because the expectation is not exact replication but rather estimation. Therefore, the mimic can coexist with that which it is mimicking while simultaneously undermining/menacing the imperial and colonial myths designed to justify their domination.

I have argued that people living on the margins of power, especially in imperial, colonial, and neocolonial contexts, will challenge centers of power in patterned ways over time and culture. The examples I have explored involve the subversion of imperial myths (that is, religiopolitical myths) used to justify and maintain claims to power. Among the premises and working assumptions I used to support this thesis are two key points made previously: (1) Dominating groups employ and perpetuate, as one strategy of dominance, myths that suggest and establish a social order (insider/outsider; powerful/powerless) and cultural hierarchy where two disparate cultures intermingle. (2) The reciprocal premise is that dominated peoples respond to these myths and their hierarchical orderings by appropriating and subverting the very myths used to dominate them. I now add a third premise: (3) Colonized peoples are in a distinctive position to shed light on the collective body of academic knowledge concerning Bible and biblical interpretation, domination and resistance, that has been traditionally been written from the perspective of the colonizer.

The three historical moments I have evaluated support my primary thesis. In each scenario, the center has employed a religiopolitical myth to justify its claims to power and, on occasion, its employment of violence.

The Dragon Slayer myth, the Spanish Guadalupan myth, and the U.S. myth of Manifest Destiny all contribute to a "setting apart" of those who are the beneficiaries of such mythological constructions. Also, in each case, the mythology suggests either implicitly or explicitly that these beneficiaries are in some manner in a privileged relationship with the protagonist deity of the myth. It is a forceful and potent claim to power whose results establish a social and cultural hierarchy for the myth's propagators and devotees.

In contrast, those who find themselves in the unfortunate position of outsiders in these mythological scenarios are viewed in a nonprivileged position in the established social order and on occasion are viewed as expendable. Reflecting on the observations of biblical scholar Burton Mack, at these points of cultural contact, the "other" in all his or her difference cannot be embraced as a remarkable human being.[23] Due to the manner in which these myths are constructed, the "other" can only be viewed as primitive and in need of development. The only recourse in this drama is to counter the mythologies used to dominate them. The "other" are in no position to meet the center's capacity for violence with retributive violence; the *mis*-distribution of power makes this scenario impossible. Rather, they tacitly conspire to alter the very discourses used to subjugate them by appropriating the myths of the dominant classes and subverting them in their own favor. To create an antimythology is as futile as armed resistance, so instead, they choose to create a countermythology that devalues the original myth while simultaneously recontextualizing and restructuring it in their favor. This form of resistance and opposition is realistic and brilliant. It has proved so effective historically that it is a phenomenon that has transcended time and cultures, as our three moments have demonstrated. I am convinced that one of the benefits of this project is that we can now compare other imperial, colonial, and neocolonial moments for parallel scenarios.

The final premise to be examined is the claim that those on the periphery are somehow in a *distinctive* hermeneutical position to appraise these encounters. I offer this assessment not because I believe the peripheral have honed the exegetical or historical methodologies to enter the debate with more precision or depth, but rather that their social location—being so unique from and counter to traditional centers of knowledge—puts them in an advantageous interpretive position in the Freirian sense.[24] Those on the periphery offer knowledge constructed from below rather than from above. The margins are *reading and writing back* at the center. Therefore, this scenario presents itself as an opportunity to look at the same data from a fresh perspective.

This reorientation of worlds and texts forces the reader to be cognizant of the long tradition of the Europeanization and Euro-Americanization of biblical interpretation that for too long has dominated the academy under the auspices of intellectual objectivity. By articulating a new point of departure—in this instance, a Chicana/o interpretation of biblical narratives and interpretations—the academic practice of traditional biblical exegesis can be scrutinized and categorized as "a class-specific cultural practice that is a fetishization of the dominating world that the text helped create."[25] More acutely, with this reorientation, I have sought to illuminate the embeddedness of "objective" biblical interpretation in the construction and justification of modern empire(s). As Fernando Segovia has thoughtfully noted,

> the enduring construct of a universal and informed reader, the reader who would attain to impartiality and objectivity through the adoption of the scientific methods and the denial of particularity and contextuality, was a praiseworthy goal but also quite naïve and dangerous. [Ultimately,] the construct remained *inherently colonialist and imperialistic.*[26]

On the "objective" nature of this cultural-specific exegetical practice, which is also a central locus for the exertion of social power and domination, Vincent Wimbush notes that

> what it represents is a challenge to the still largely unacknowledged interested, invested, racialized, culture- and ethnic-specific practice of biblical interpretation that is part of an even larger pattern of such interpretation of literatures and of history in the West. Incredibly, there are some even today within academic professional circles and within popular religious discourses who fervently claim that their particular brand of interpretation ("exegesis") is

consistently carried out in (a scientific or disciplined or fair-minded) neutral key or mode.[27]

As a counterdiscourse to those "traditional" (European, Euro-American, "objective") interpretations, therefore, I took as my point of departure "*a different time*, which means from a *different site of interpretation and enunciation*, with the necessary correlative *different presuppositions, orientations and agenda*."[28] I began with a social location, my social location, as a member of a group of people who call themselves Chicanas/os. Therefore, I offer this socially located reading also as a challenge to the contemporary guild of biblical studies in the manner expressed by Wimbush:

> It argues that the point of departure for and even the crux of interpretation not be texts but worlds, viz. society and culture and the complex textu(r)alizations of society and culture. Further, it argues that this point of departure should begin in a different time—not with the (biblical) past but with the present, that is with the effort to understand how the present is being shaped by the Bible (which then provides for forays into the past).[29]

Therefore, as Segovia contends that

> with readers now fully foregrounding themselves as flesh-and-blood readers, variously situated and engaged in their own respective social locations, the process of liberation and decolonization moves into the sociocultural domain itself. . . . Such a reading takes competing modes of discourse for granted, renounces the idea of any master narrative as in itself a construct, and looks for a truly global interaction . . . [creating] a world in which readers become as important as texts and in which models and reconstructions are regarded as constructions.[30]

The process of relocating our interpretive points of departure from texts to our distinctive social locations is not simply an intellectual enterprise but is the primary impetus for the construction of discourses that initiate the process of liberation and decolonialization. Rather than promoting the continued "silencing" of critical readings of both worlds and texts, a recentered engagement of Bible and biblical interpretations foregrounds provocative readings of Bible that first and foremost recognize the interpretive capacity to be "the consistent clarion and provocation for disruption and disconnection, critique and challenge[.] Who handling it will not come to read it as a road map for exiting, for de-formation and re-formation?"[31] In these cultural sites of re-formation, the creation of third, interstitial, and border spaces is most evident.

As a result, I locate the argument of the preceding chapters squarely in the camp of postcolonial biblical studies because I have placed the issue of colonialism at the center of my approach to the Bible and its interpretation. I have focused on the justifications for expansion and domination as central forces in the interpretation of biblical narratives. Challenging the interpretations of the center by recognizing and exposing oppression and misrepresentations can contribute to a more just world by fostering noncoercive knowledge produced in the interest of human liberation.

Like liberation criticism, postcolonial biblical criticism emerged in the Third World, with both disciplines sharing the same emancipatory ideals. Postcolonial biblical criticism, however, is "deeply suspicious of the liberationist tendency to give the Bible the unquestioned benefit of the doubt, to regard the Bible itself as *the* place where the message of liberation is to be found."[32] Therefore, postcolonial biblical critics are quick to remind liberationist hermeneuts, "The Bible arrived in the hands of the colonizer, who saw it as an indispensable means with which the colonized were to be civilized."[33] Vincent Wimbush, therefore, rightly emphasizes, "The 'Bible' . . . clearly cannot be understood as a transcendent, ahistorical force; it must be seen as a decidedly sociocultural, political, historical construction but as such a nonetheless dangerous and powerful force."[34] Theologies of liberation need to be critically assessed as subversions of dominant myths rather than to be employed as *the* critical interpretive model. Theologies of liberation make explicit claims to a privileged relationship with a deity. To posit as a primary assumption that God has a "preferential option for the poor" is to argue that God advocates for the poor against the imperial, colonial, and neocolonial centers. It therefore subverts the ideologies used to oppress those who are at the margins of society. Only when we as collective interpreters of Bible come to recognize the role that Christian Scripture and scriptural interpretations have played in the long and complex history of imperial, colonial, and neocolonial enterprises can the process of liberation truly begin. Biblical texts themselves must be subject to the careful and critical scrutiny to which biblical interpretations have been exposed.

Finally, I hope to have made a contribution to the body of literature that identifies the Iberian Peninsula and 1492 as the foundational moment of modernity when Europe was first in position to pose itself against an "other." Only from this starting point will we collectively be able to welcome that *first* "other"—the indigenous peoples of Latin America (in this case, specifically Mexico) and, by extension, the Chicanas/os of the United States—into the larger postcolonial conversation.

APPENDIX 1

TEXTS OF THE GUADALUPE TRADITION

THE SPANISH TEXTUAL TRADITION

The various Spanish versions recount the same basic story of the Virgin's apparition in Spain, differing only in certain minor details. The basic tenor of all these accounts champion the cause of the independent Spanish states against the Arab-Islamic nomads who had occupied much of Spain, employing the Marian apparition as the sign of her advocacy. Thus, these Spanish versions participate in and contribute to the emerging spirit of reconquista, which in the sixteenth century was transferred to the Americas during the conquest of Mexico.

Codex written before 1400, now missing

Codex 555 of the Archivo Histórico Nacional (1440)

Codex of Father Alonso de la Rambla (1484)

Codex 344 of the Archivo Histórico Nacional (1500)

Codex of Father Diego de Ecija (died 1534)

Codex of Father Juan Herrera (1535)
(now in the Library of the Escorial, IV-a-10)

THE MEXICAN GUADALUPE TRADITION

We can say nothing with certainty regarding a possible indigenous oral tradition, or regarding the *Nican mopohua* appearing in the sixteenth century (see the discussion in chapter 3). The extant Mexican Guadalupe tradition derives from the seventeenth century with the works of Sánchez and de la Vega. This tradition involves the Creole (and perhaps indigenous) subversion of older Spanish mythology.

Disputed indigenous oral tradition (sixteenth century?)

Nican mopohua (sixteenth century?)[1]

Miguel Sanchez's *Imagen de la Virgen María* (1648)

Luis Laso de la Vega's *Huei tlamahuiçoltica* (1649)

Mateo de la Cruz's *Relación de la milagrosa aparición de la Santa Virgen de Guadalupe* (1662)

APPENDIX 2

EL PLAN ESPIRITUAL DE AZTLÁN[1]

The Plan Espiritual de Aztlán *was adopted by the First National Chicano Youth Liberation Conference in Denver in 1969; the document is in the public domain.*

In the spirit of a new people that is conscious not only of its proud historical heritage but also of the brutal "Gringo" invasion of our territories: we, the Chicano inhabitants and civilizers of the northern land of Aztlán, from whence came our forefathers, reclaiming the land of their birth and consecrating the determination of our people of the sun, declare our power, our responsibility, and our inevitable destiny.

We are free and sovereign to determine those tasks which are justly called for by our house, our land, the sweat of our brows and by our hearts. Aztlán belongs to those who plant the seeds, water the fields, and gather the crops, and not to the foreign Europeans. We do not recognize capricious frontiers on the Bronze Continent.

Brotherhood unites and love for our brothers makes us a people whose time has come and who struggle against the foreigner "Gabacho,"[2] who exploits our riches and destroys our culture. With our heart in our hands and our hands in the soil, We declare the independence of our Mestizo[3] Nation. We are a Bronze People with a Bronze Culture. Before the world, before all of North America, before all our brothers in the Bronze Continent, We are a Nation, we are a Union of Free Pueblos,[4] we are Aztlán.

Por La Raza todo. Fuera de La Raza nada.[5]

PROGRAM

El Plan Espiritual de Aztlán sets the theme that the Chicanos (La Raza de Bronze) must use their nationalism as the key or common denominator for mass mobilization and organization. Once we are committed to the idea and philosophy of El Plan de Aztlán, we can only conclude that social, economic, cultural, and political independence is the only road to total liberation from oppression, exploitation, and racism. Our struggle then must be for the control of our barrios, campos,[6] pueblos, lands, our economy, our culture, and our political life. El Plan commits all levels of Chicano society—the barrio, the campo, the ranchero, the writer, the teacher, the worker, the professional—to La Causa.

NATIONALISM

Nationalism as the key to organization transcends all religious, political, class, and economic factions or boundaries. Nationalism is the common denominator that all members of La Raza can agree upon.

ORGANIZATIONAL GOALS

1. **UNITY** in the thinking of our people concerning the barrios, the pueblo, the campo, the land, the poor, the middle class, the professional—all committed to the liberation of La Raza.
2. **ECONOMY:** economic control of our lives and our communities can only come about by driving the exploiter out of our communities, our pueblos, and our lands and by controlling and developing our own talents, sweat, and resources. Cultural background and values which ignore materialism and embrace humanism will contribute to the act of cooperative buying and the distribution of resources and production to sustain an economic base for healthy growth and development. Lands rightfully ours will be fought for and defended. Land and realty ownership will be acquired by the community for the people's welfare. Economic ties of responsibility must be secured by nationalism and the Chicano defense units.
3. **EDUCATION** must be relative to our people, i.e., history, culture, bilingual education, contributions, etc. Community control of our

schools, our teachers, our administrators, our counselors, and our programs.

4. **INSTITUTIONS** shall serve our people by providing the service necessary for a full life and their welfare on the basis of restitution, not handouts or beggar's crumbs. Restitution for past economic slavery, political exploitation, ethnic and cultural psychological destruction and denial of civil and human rights. Institutions in our community which do not serve the people have no place in the community. The institutions belong to the people.

5. **SELF-DEFENSE** of the community must rely on the combined strength of the people. The front line defense will come from the barrios, the campos, the pueblos, and the ranchitos. Their involvement as protectors of their people will be given respect and dignity. They in turn offer their responsibility and their lives for their people. Those who place themselves in the front ranks for their people do so out of love and carnalismo.[7] Those institutions which are fattened by our brothers to provide employment and political pork barrels for the gringo will do so only as acts of liberation and for La Causa. For the very young there will no longer be acts of juvenile delinquency but revolutionary acts.

6. **CULTURAL** values of our people strengthen our identity and the moral backbone of the movement. Our culture unites and educates the family of La Raza towards liberation with one heart and one mind. We must ensure that our writers, poets, musicians, and artists produce literature and art that is appealing to our people and relates to our revolutionary culture. Our cultural values of life, family, and home will serve as a powerful weapon to defeat the gringo dollar value system and encourage the process of love and brotherhood.

7. **POLITICAL LIBERATION** can only come through independent action on our part, since the two-party system is the same animal with two heads that feed from the same trough. Where we are a majority, we will control; where we are a minority, we will represent a pressure group; nationally, we will represent one party: La Familia de La Raza!

ACTION

1. Awareness and distribution of El Plan Espiritual de Aztlán. Presented at every meeting, demonstration, confrontation, courthouse, institution, administration, church, school, tree, building, car, and every place of human existence.

2. September 16, on the birthdate of Mexican Independence, a national walk-out by all Chicanos of all colleges and schools to be sustained until the complete revision of the educational system: its policy makers, administration, its curriculum, and its personnel to meet the needs of our community.

3. Self-defense against the occupying forces of the oppressors at every school, every available man, woman, and child.

4. Community nationalization and organization of all Chicanos: El Plan Espiritual de Aztlán.

5. Economic program to drive the exploiter out of our community and a welding together of our people's combined resources to control their own production through cooperative effort.

6. Creation of an independent local, regional, and national political party.

A nation autonomous and free—culturally, socially, economically, and politically—will make its own decisions on the usage of our lands, the taxation of our goods, the utilization of our bodies for war, the determination of justice (reward and punishment), and the profit of our sweat.

El Plan de Aztlán is the plan of liberation!

APPENDIX 3

THE VIRGIN OF GUADALUPE IN THE MURALS OF EAST LOS ANGELES

Plate 1. The Virgin of Guadalupe, Estremadura, Spain. This statuette of the Virgin with Jesus has been housed continuously in a national cathedral in the region of Estremadura since 1340, some 180 years before the traditional Mexican apparition story. The cathedral was the site of the commissioning of Columbus by Fernando and Isabel before his first journey to the Americas. The region of Estremadura was also home to many of the first Spanish conquistadores, including Hernán Cortés. According to Spanish mythological tradition, the statuette was carved by Saint Luke. Image copyright © Real Monesterio de Nuestra Señora de Guadalupe, Estremadura. Used by permission.

N. S. de Guadalupe, Patrona de Mexᶜᵒ y de la Nueva España, tocada á lõ Sagrado Original, el dia 6 de Marzo, de 1766. Adevᵒ de Dⁿ Blas Antonie de Orio.

Plate 2. The Virgin of Guadalupe, Tepeyac, Mexico. According to Mexican tradition, this was the tilma (outer garment) worn by Juan Diego when the Virgin Mary appeared to him on a hill just outside of modern Mexico City (Tepeyac). The image on the tilma was left miraculously by the Virgin Mary as proof for the doubting Spanish clergy that she had appeared to Juan Diego. Note the profound differences between the Spanish and Mexican versions of Guadalupe, especially the lack of the Christ child and the Mexican rendition's affinity to the woman described in Revelation 12. The Virgin of Guadalupe is supported by an angel in this image. Image copyright © Christie's Images/CORBIS. Used by permission.

Plate 3. A home on Rowan Avenue, East Los Angeles. Here the crowned Virgin of Guadalupe is fixed prominently outside a devotee's home, with an *altarcito* (a little altar) holding flowers.

Plate 4. A home on Findlay Avenue, Montebello. This tiled Virgin of Guadalupe was placed under the window of a young female child who was stricken with leukemia. The role of Guadalupe as protector of the suffering is highlighted.

Plate 5. Bodega, Avenida César Chávez, East Los Angeles. This storefront mural is employed by a neighborhood healer/healing center. Note the depiction of the Jesus child—similar to the original Spanish icon (see Plate 1). This mural also includes crowns for both the Virgin of Guadalupe and Jesus.

Plate 6. One of dozens of murals in the Estrada Courts Housing Project, East Los Angeles. The lack of graffiti on this wall in an especially acute gang environment is an indication of the reverence in which the Virgin of Guadalupe is held. Steve Delgado, artist (1973).

Plate 7. Ramona Gardens Housing Project, East Los Angeles. Here again, the Virgin of Guadalupe finds a home in a depressed housing project in the Boyle Heights section of East Los Angeles. Armando Cabrera, artist (1974); reworked by Joe Rodriguez (date unknown).

Plate 8. Mural of Guadalupe, Maravilla Housing Project, Avenida César Chávez and Mednik Avenue, East Los Angeles. Housing projects in East Los Angeles are reserved primarily for Mexican and Chicana/o low-income families (i.e., the marginalized) and can be likened to indigenous reservations in that they are federally subsidized and ethnically homogeneous. The Maravilla Housing Project sat at the epicenter of the 1970 East Los Angeles riots. David Lopez and Sam Zepeda (1973).

Plate 9. Estrada Courts Housing Project, East Los Angeles. This mural is an example of the ethnic demeanor and posture of resistance that characterize many of the murals in this housing project. Note the image of Latin American revolutionary Che Guevara. *Congresso of Artistas: Cosmicos d' las Americas d' San Diego Califaz:* Mario Torero, El Lton, Zade artists (1978).

Plate 10. C & C Market, 8th Street and Concord Avenue, East Los Angeles. This is one of the few murals of the Virgin of Guadalupe that have been defaced by graffiti. Observe, however, that the graffiti does not touch the figure of the Virgin of Guadalupe, nor does the proprietor's attempt to cover the graffiti. Note also the crown, which is not found on the original Mexican Virgin of Guadalupe. The crown connects this mural more closely to the Queen of Heaven described in Revelation 12.

Plate 11. Jubilee 2000 Mural, Our Lady Queen of the Angels Church, Los Angeles. This mural is located at one of the most immigrant-friendly churches in all of Los Angeles. The caption above the Virgin of Guadalupe reads, "Queen of Mexico and Empress of America." The mural is adorned by all the flags of South and Central America, Mexico, and the United States. All flags fly in the dominant left-to-right position (according to U.S. military protocol) with the exception of the U.S. flag, which is in the submissive right-to-left position. E. J. Harpham and Pacific Tilescopes, artist and creator (2000).

Plate 12. Rico's Taco Restaurant, Los Angeles. The flags of Mexico and the United States are incorporated into the mural. As in Plate 11, the U.S. flag is displayed in the submissive right-to-left position and farther from the Virgin of Guadalupe than its Mexican counterpart. Note also the depiction of the indigenous Juan Diego.

Plate 13. Avenida César Chávez, East Los Angeles. The mural on this establishment features Juan Diego with the Virgin of Guadalupe, highlighting the indigenous component of the apparition myth. It also adds the crown not featured in the Mexican original but consistent with Revelation 12. Note also the flower offerings at the foot of the Virgin. Such sites are known as altarcitos (little altars) by local devotees (*Guadalupanas/os*).

Plate 14. Virgin's Seed, La Casa Market, Hammel and Hazard Streets, East Los Angeles. This colorful rendition of the Virgin of Guadalupe also adds the crown to the original Mexican icon, and includes the eagle and serpent motif found on the national flag of Mexico, as described in Aztec (Mexica) foundational myths. Paul Botello, artist; Isabel Moral, assistant volunteer (1991).

Plate 15. Zamora Carneceria (meat market), Avenida César Chávez, East Los Angeles. This mural also adds the crown on the Virgin of Guadalupe, and the indigenous Juan Diego. This mural has been partially defaced by the addition of a restraining wall that makes contact with the Virgin of Guadalupe's hem.

Plate 16. Mural on carniceria Avenida César Chávez, East Los Angeles. There is proximate graffiti on the trash bin but not on the establishment's wall with the Virgin of Guadalupe.

Plate 17. El Mercado Parking Lot, First Street, East Los Angeles. This tile representation of Guadalupe is located in one of East Los Angeles' most prominent shopping venues, *El Mercado* (The Market). Commonly frequented by recent immigrants, this shopping area maintains the flavor of Mexico in its products for sale and its food courts. Note the no-parking area directly in front of the shrine, the extensive *altarcito*, and the elaborate adornment.

Plate 18. Downey Auto Center, Downey and Olympic Boulevards, East Los Angeles. Even an "auto center" wall claims a significant space for the Virgin of Guadalupe. Of special interest here are the votive and flower offerings of the altarcito, the added crown, and the ornate lighting of the shrine. Note the light bulb in front of the head of the Virgin of Guadalupe for night viewing.

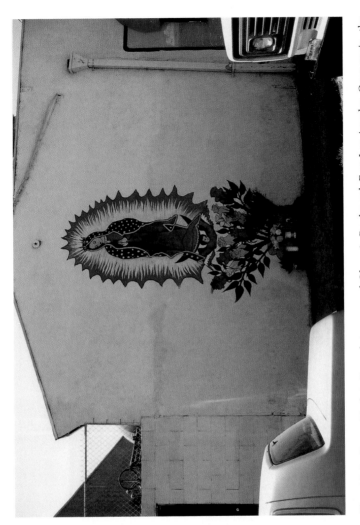

Plate 19. La Sirena Market, Record Avenue and Olympic Boulevard, East Los Angeles. Once again, the crown is added to this mural, and a small *altarcito* is featured.

Plate 20. Mozart Street, Lincoln Heights, East Los Angeles. This depiction of the Virgin of Guadalupe is striking in its juxtaposition to the scantily clad "Fanta Girls." It is distinctive of the barrio that the sacred and the profane both find their home here, and that the sacred is often prominent.

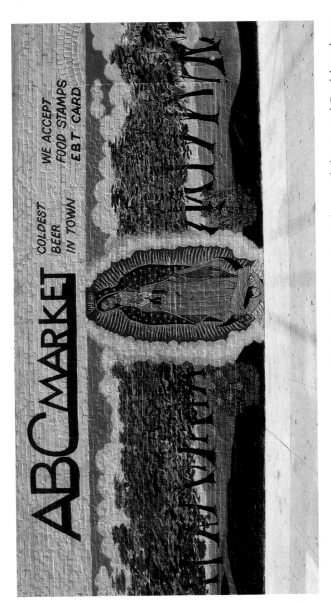

Plate 21. ABC Market, Manitou Avenue, Lincoln Heights, East Los Angeles. In this mural, the crowned Guadalupe shares wall space with an advertisement for the "Coldest Beer in Town," again juxtaposing the sacred and the profane. Devotees will on occasion offer beer libations to the Virgin of Guadalupe at *altarcitos*. The economic status of the barrio is suggested by the announcement "We Accept Food Stamps."

Plate 22. Hermana Milagros (Sister Miracles), Spiritualist, Avenida César Chávez, East Los Angeles. It should be noted that the barrio's employment of the Virgin of Guadalupe transcends "traditional" Catholic applications. Here a neighborhood healer (*curandera*) employs the iconography on her business. The banner at the front of the establishment reads, "Sister Miracles; We Resolve Whatever Problem; We Read the Past, Present and Future; We Clean Your Bad Luck; Specialist of Love." The sign that incorporates the Virgin reads, "Free Cleanings Performed."

Plate 23. Automobile, Arizona Avenue, East Los Angeles. Images of Guadalupe are not restricted to walls in the barrio. Here a decal of the Virgin of Guadalupe is placed on the rear window of a vehicle. The Virgin of Guadalupe is an important icon for the journeyer, especially for those traveling from Latin America to the United States. (She is the protector of travelers to foreign and sometimes hostile lands.)

Plate 24. Van, Rowan Avenue, East Los Angeles. Another working-class vehicle displays the Virgin of Guadalupe prominently.

Plate 25. Taco truck, First Street, East Los Angeles. In this mural, the icon of the Virgin of Guadalupe has been imported into a scene from the proprietor's hometown, Guadalajara, Mexico, thereby highlighting the association between image and place. The placement of the Virgin of Guadalupe in restaurants and other eateries is common in East Los Angeles and in Mexico.

Plate 26. This tiled statuette is located outside of the Mexican and Chicana/o artists' haven known as Self Help Graphics Avenida César Chávez, East Los Angeles. The Virgin of Guadalupe remains at the forefront of barrio artists' minds some thirty-five years after the apex of the Chicana/o movement. Although the symbol is multivalent, it remains a potential locus of resistance in Mexican and Chicana/o appropriations. Recent deployments of the Virgin of Guadalupe at pro-immigration rallies attest to this spontaneous and ongoing potentiality.

ABBREVIATIONS

ABD	*Anchor Bible Dictionary*
AJ	*Art Journal*
AKGWG	Abhandlungen der königlichen Gesellschaft der Wissenschaften zu Göttingen, Phil.-hist. Kl., N.F.
AUSS	*Andrews University Seminary Studies*
BDV	*Bulletin Dei Verbum*
BR	Biblical Research
CBQ	Catholic Biblical Quarterly
HNT	Handbuch zum Neuen Testament
HTR	*Harvard Theological Review*
HTS	Harvard Theological Studies
JAAR	*Journal of the American Academy of Religion*
JBL	*Journal of Biblical Literature*
JSNT	Journal for the Study of the New Testament
JSNTSup	Journal for the Study of the New Testament: Supplement Series
KEK	Kristisch-exegetischer Kommentar über das Neue Testament (Meyer-Kommentar)
LCL	Loeb Classical Library
LQ	Lutheran Quarterly
MLN	Modern Language Notes
NTS	New Testament Studies
OLR	*Oxford Literary Review*

RGRW	Religions in the Graeco-Roman World
RQ	Restoration Quarterly
RThom	Revue thomiste
SBLMS	Society of Biblical Literature Monograph Series
SNTSMS	Society for New Testament Studies Monograph Series
TS	*Theological Studies*
TU	Texte und Untersuchungen
WBC	Word Biblical Commentary
WTJ	Westminster Theological Journal

NOTES

INTRODUCTION

1. I do not use these two terms synonymously. Here *Mexican* will refer to those people of Mexican ancestry born in Mexico. I use the terms *Chicanas* and *Chicanos* specifically for those people of Mexican ancestry born in the United States, who are sometimes also referred to as Mexican-Americans. The term *Chicana/o* here is both an ethnic and a sociopolitical designation. For more on this matter, see pp. 94–5 below.

2. See James C. Scott, *Weapons of the Weak: Everyday Forms of Peasant Resistance* (New Haven: Yale University Press, 1985).

3. James C. Scott, *Domination and the Arts of Resistance: Hidden Transcripts* (New Haven: Yale University Press, 1990), xii.

4. On this matter, see R. S. Sugirtharajah, *Postcolonial Criticism and Biblical Interpretation* (Oxford: Oxford University Press, 2002), 53.

5. Robert Schreiter, *Constructing Local Theologies* (Maryknoll, N.Y.: Orbis, 1985), 136–7.

6. See Scott, *Domination and the Arts of Resistance*, xii.

7. Vincent Wimbush, *Introduction: Interpreting Resistance, Resisting Interpretations*, pp. 1–10 in *Semeia* (1997), here p. 6.

8. On the issue of cross-historical comparisons of power and resistance, see ibid., 3. Wimbush argues in this way:

> Do the most basic dynamics of human power relations as some of us have experienced them—gaining and wielding power, being overpowered, using power to dominate others, resisting domination—really change over time? A presupposition that motored our investigation is that the most basic of power dynamics are probably perduring.

9. This myth was commonly known in antiquity as the Leto-Python-Apollo Myth.

10. *El Plan Espiritual de Aztlán* (*The Spiritual Plan of Aztlán*) was composed at the First National Chicano Youth Liberation Conference in Denver. See Appendix 2.

11. The Dragon Slayer myth is this section's focus, but it is not, however, my contention that this is the only ancient Near Eastern myth embedded in Revelation 12. What makes this text so wonderfully elusive is the author's weaving of several ancient myths into the text, thus making literal translations or comparisons much more difficult. Rather, the echoes or subtle suggestions pique the curiosity of the Christian reader and keep the non-Christian reader off balance. Revelation 12 is, in the truest sense, a powerful example of an *art of resistance*. It should also be noted that the Dragon Slayer myth has been chosen as this section's focus because of its relevance for construction of later imperial ideologies, especially Augustan.

12. D. A. Brading, *Mexican Phoenix: Our Lady of Guadalupe: Image and Tradition Across Five Centuries* (Cambridge: Cambridge University Press, 2001), 5.

13. This observation is credited to Jean-Pierre Ruiz, "The Bible and U.S. Hispanic American Theological Discourse: Lessons from a Non-Innocent History," in *From the Heart of Our People: Latino/a Explorations in Catholic Systematic Theology*, ed. Orlando O. Espín and Miguel H. Díaz (Maryknoll: Orbis, 1999), 107. Here Ruiz refers to Patricia Harrington's "Mother of Death, Mother of Rebirth: The Mexican Virgin of Guadalupe," *JAAR* 56/1 (1988): 35–7. See also Jonathan Brown, *Images and Ideas in Seventeenth Century Spanish Painting* (Princeton: Princeton University Press, 1978).

14. Enrique Dussel, "Eurocentrism and Modernity (Introduction to the Frankfurt Lectures)," in *The Postmodernism Debate in Latin America*, ed. Michael Aronna, John Beverley, and José Oviedo (Durham, N.C.: Duke University Press, 1995), 65.

15. Sugirtharajah. *Postcolonial Criticism and Biblical Interpretation*, 25.

16. Ibid., 40.

17. Eduard Said, *The World, the Text, and the Critic* (Cambridge, Mass.: Harvard University Press, 1983), 29.

18. Bill Ashcroft, Gareth Griffiths, and Helen Tiffin, *Post-Colonial Studies: The Key Concepts* (New York: Routledge, 2000), 118 and 139.

19. Ibid., 193.

20. Ibid., 12–13.

21. Ibid., 118.

22. Scott, *Domination and the Arts of Resistance*, xii, 2–3.

23. Ibid., xvi.

24. I use the term *imperial myth* here in the cosmological sense, referring specifically to the way these myths function in justifying claims of imperial and colonial power and in the ongoing maintenance of such power. In contrast, responses to dominant myths I refer to as mythological subversions or countermyths.

25. Dussel, "Eurocentrism and Modernity," 67.

CHAPTER 1: FIRST-CENTURY ASIA MINOR

1. The myth is technically known as the Isis-Horus-Seth/Typhon myth and the Egyptian form of the myth can be summarized in the most general of terms as follows: Typhon murders Osiris the husband/brother of Isis; Isis recovers the body of Osiris which had been cut into 14 separate pieces and scattered by Seth/Typhon (with the exception of the Osiris' phallus which is replaced by an artificial phallus); after the resurrection of Osiris, Isis becomes impregnated by Osiris and gives birth to a son named Horus; Osiris descends to the Underworld; Seth/Typhon pursues Isis and Horus; Horus overcomes Seth/Typhon; Horus is established as ruler.

2. On this matter, see David E. Aune, *Revelation 6–16* (WBC 52B; Nashville: Thomas Nelson, 1998), 670; Adela Yarbro Collins, *The Combat Myth in the Book of Revelation* (1976; repr., Eugene, Ore: Wipf and Stock, 2001), 65; Joseph Fontenrose, *Python: A Study in Delphic Myth and Its Origins* (Berkeley: University of California Press, 1959), 210; W. K. Hedrick, "The Sources and Use of Imagery in Apocalypse 12" (Ph.D. diss., Berkeley: Graduate Theological Union, 1970), 99.

3. Mary Grant, trans. and ed., *The Myths of Hyginus* (Lawrence: University of Kansas Press, 1960), 115–16.

4. Hesiod, "Homeric Hymns III (to Delian Apollo) and IV (to Pythian Apollo)," in *The Homeric Hymns*, trans. Hugh G. Evelyn-White (LCL; New York: Macmillan, 1914).

5. Theogonis, lines 1–10, in E. Harrison, *Studies in Theogonis* (Cambridge: Cambridge University Press, 1902).

6. Pindar, "Processional Song: On Delos," in *The Odes of Pindar*, trans. John Sandys (LCL; Cambridge, Mass.: Harvard University Press, 1961).

7. Herodotus, "Herodotus II," in *Herodotus*, trans. A. D. Godley (LCL 1; New York: Putnam's Sons, 1921).

8. Euripides, "Iphegenia in Taurus," in *Euripides*, trans. A. S. Way (LCL 2; New York: Macmillan, 1912).

9. Callimachus, "Hymn to Apollo and Hymn to Delos," in *Callimachus, Lycophron, Aratus*, trans. A. W. Mair (LCL; Cambridge, Mass.: Harvard University Press, 1960).

10. Apollodorus 1.4.1, in *Apollodorus, The Library*, trans. James G. Frazer (LCL; Cambridge, Mass.: Harvard University Press, 1961).

11. Plutarch, "On Isis and Osiris" and "On the Obsolescence of Oracles," in *Moralia*, trans. F. C. Babbitt (LCL 5; Cambridge, Mass.: Harvard University Press, 1962).

12. Pausanias 2.7.7; 2.30.3; 10.6.5; and 10.7.2, in *Pausanias, Description of Greece*, trans. W. H. S. Jones (LCL; Cambridge, Mass.: Harvard University Press, 1964).

13. Lucian, "Dialogues of the Sea Gods 9 (10)," in *Lucian*, trans. M. D. Macleod (LCL 7; Cambridge, Mass.: Harvard University Press, 1961).

14. Lucian, 5.78–81.

15. For a complete and detailed survey of these accounts, see Hedrick, "The Sources and Use of Imagery in Apocalypse 12," esp. pp. 102–8. His survey is taken from Theodor Schreiber, *Apollon Pythoktonos: Ein Beitrag zur griechischen Religions- und Kunstgeschichte* (Leipzig: Engelmann, 1879).

16. Schreiber, *Apollon Pythoktonos*, 90–5.

17. Hedrick, "The Sources and Use of Imagery," 110.

18. Schreiber, *Apollon Pythoktonos*, 79–85.

19. Hedrick, "The Sources and Use of Imagery," 112.

20. See Yarbro Collins, *Combat Myth*, 245–61.

21. Paul Zanker, *The Power of Images in the Age of Augustus*, trans. Alan Shapiro, (Ann Arbor: University of Michigan Press, 1990), 47.

22. "Already as a boy [it was claimed that] he had superhuman powers, and even frogs obeyed his commands. . . . A number of dreams and omens associated the youth with the sun and stars." Zanker, *Power of Images*, 47–8.

23. For a later example of Augustan propaganda, see Augustus Caesar, "Res Gestae Divi Augusti," 12ff., 24–7, 34ff., in *The New Testament Background: Writings from Ancient Greece and the Roman Empire That Illuminate Christian Origins*, ed. C. K. Barrett (San Francisco: Harper San Francisco, 1989), 1–5.

24. Zanker, *Power of Images*, 48–9.

25. Suetonius, *Lives of the Caesars: The Deified Augustus*, 50. Quoted from: *Suetonius Volume 1*; Loeb Classical Library; John C. Rolfe, ed. and trans. Cambridge: Harvard University Press, 1998 (rev. w/new intro.), p. 229.

26. Zanker, *Power of Images*, 50.

27. Ibid., 50.

28. Ibid., 51.

29. Hedrick, "The Sources and Use of Imagery," 148–9.

30. Ibid., 149.

31. Yarbro Collins, *Combat Myth*, 189.

32. Eugene M. Boring, *Revelation* (Louisville: John Knox, 1989), 151.

33. All Biblical citations are NRSV translations unless otherwise specified.

34. Eberhard Vischer, *Die Offenbarung Johannis: Eine jüdische Apokalypse in christlicher Bearbeitung* (TU 2/3; Leipzig: Hinrichs, 1886), 19–27.

35. G. J. Vischer, *Omwerkings en Compilatie-Hypothesen toegepast op de Apokalypse van Johannes* (Groningen: Wolters, 1888).

36. Friedrich Spitta, *Die Offenbarung des Johannes* (Halle: Waisenhaus, 1889), 125–7; Johannes Weiss, ed. *Offenbarung des Johannes in Die Schriften des Neuen Testaments* (Göttingen: Vandenhoeck & Ruprecht, 1908); Julius Wellhausen, *Analyse der Offenbarung Johannis* (AkGWG, N.F. 9/4; Berlin: Weidmann, 1907); and Yarbro Collins, *Combat Myth*, 104–7.

37. Wilhelm Bousset, *Die Offenbarung Johannis* (6 ed.; Göttingen: Vandenhoeck & Ruprecht, 1906); and Ernst Lohmeyer, *Die Offenbarung des Johannes* (HNT 16; Tübingen: Mohr [Siebeck], 1926).

38. Yarbro Collins, *Combat Myth*, 104 (emphasis added).

39. Ibid., 105.

40. Ibid.

41. Ibid., 107.

42. There also existed messianic expectation without the explicit use of the term *messiah* in some of the ancient literature, and there was also a trajectory of eschatological expectation in Judaism that focused entirely on God as agent (see *Jubilees* 23; Baruch 2:34ff., 4:36ff., 5:5ff.; Tobit 13:11ff., 14:4ff; and *Assumption of Moses* 10:1ff.).

43. James Charlesworth, ed., *The Messiah: Developments in Earliest Judaism and Christianity* (Minneapolis: Fortress Press, 1992), xv.

44. For similar cautionary arguments, see Merrill P. Miller, "The Problems of the Origins of a Messianic Jesus," in *Redescribing Christian Origins*, ed. Ron Cameron and Merrill P. Miller (Atlanta: Society of Biblical Literature, 2004); Oscar Cullman, *The Christology of the New Testament* (London: SCM, 1959); Jacob Neusner et al., *Judaisms and Their Messiahs at the Turn of the Christian Century* (Cambridge: Cambridge University Press, 1987); Gerd Theissen and Annette Merz, *Jesus als historische Gestalt: Beiträge zur Jesusforschung* (Göttingen: Vandenhoeck & Ruprecht, 2003); and Richard A. Horsley, "Messianic Figures and Movements in First-Century Palestine," in *The Messiah: Developments in Earliest Judaism and Christianity*, ed. James Charlesworth (Minneapolis: Fortress Press, 1992), 276–95.

45. Horsley, "Messianic Figures," 276-281 and 293-295.

46. See especially John J. Collins, *The Scepter and the Star: The Messiahs of the Dead Sea Scrolls and Other Ancient Literature* (New York: Doubleday, 1995); and James D. G. Dunn, *Jesus Remembered* (Grand Rapids: Eerdmans, 2003). Although I refer to these two scholars' position as one of compromise, I do believe that their conclusions are also overstated, for example, when Dunn states, "We can extend Collins's conclusion with some confidence that the hope of a royal Messiah was *widespread* among the unlettered masses" (*Jesus Remembered*, 621).

47. See J. Collins, *The Scepter and the Star*, 22–48.

48. Here Dunn cites *The Old Testament Pseudepigraha*, ed. J. H. Charlesworth (London: Darton; 2 vols. 1983, 1985).

49. *Pss.* Sol. 17:32 and similarly 18:5-7.

50. Dunn, *Jesus Remembered*, 620. The relevant citations are 1QS 9:11; CD 12:23—13:1; 14:19; 19:10-11; 20:1. On the dual messiahship, see J. Collins, *The Scepter and the Star*, 74–83.

51. Gerd Theissen and Annette Merz, *The Historical Jesus: A Comprehensive Guide* (Minneapolis: Fortress Press, 1996), 538.

52. J. Collins, *The Scepter and the Star*, 36 (emphasis added).

53. Dunn, *Jesus Remembered*, 621. See also Acts 1:6.

54. J. Collins, *The Scepter and the Star*, 95. See also Stefan Schreiber, *Gesalbter und König: Titel und Konzeptionen der königlichen Gesalbterwerwartung in frühjüdischen und urchristlichen Schriften* (Berlin: de Gruyter, 2000), 541–2.

55. Theissen and Merz, *The Historical Jesus*, 537.

56. Yarbro Collins, *Combat Myth*, 128.

57. Victor Tcherikover, *Hellenistic Civilization and the Jews* (Philadelphia: Jewish Publication Society of America, 1959), 296–7 (emphasis added).

58. Philip A. Harland, *Associations, Synagogues, and Congregations: Claiming a Space in Ancient Mediterranean Society* (Minneapolis: Fortress Press, 2003), 11.

59. Modern proponents of this model include but are not limited to John A.Elliot, *A Home for the Homeless: A Social-Scientific Criticism of 1 Peter, Its Situation and Strategy* (2nd ed.; Minneapolis: Fortress Press, 1990); Harry O. Meier, *The Social Setting of the Ministry as Reflected in the Writings of Hermas, Clement and Ignatius* (Waterloo, Ontario: Wilfred Laurier University Press, 1991); Margaret Y. MacDonald, *A Socio-historical Study of Institutionalization in the Pauline and Deutero-Pauline Writings* (SNTSMS 60; Cambridge: Cambridge University Press, 1988); Wayne Meeks, *The First Urban Christians: The Social World of the Apostle Paul* (New Haven: Yale University Press, 1983); E. Mary Smallwood, *The Jews under Roman Rule: From Pompey to Diocletian* (Leiden: Brill, 1976); and M. Weber, *Ancient Judaism* (New York: Free Press, 1952).

60. Harland, *Associations, Synagogues, and Congregations*, 177–8, 191.

61. For comparable studies of a more accommodating diaspora Judaism, see Paul R. Trebilco, *Jewish Communities in Asia Minor* (Cambridge: Cambridge University Press, 1991); A. T. Krabel, "Judaism in Western Asia Minor under the Roman Empire, with a Preliminary Study of the Jewish Community at Sardis, Lydia" (Diss., Harvard University, 1968); David A. Balch, *Let Wives Be Submissive: The Domestic Code in 1 Peter* (SBLMS 26; Chico, Calif.: Scholars, 1981); and David A. Balch, "Hellenization/Acculturation in 1 Peter," in *Perspectives on First Peter* (Macon, Ga.: Mercer University Press, 1986), 79–101.

62. Harland, *Associations, Synagogues, and Congregations*, 178.

63. Ibid., 200.

64. Trebilco, *Jewish Communities*, 187.

65. Ibid., 186.

66. Harland, *Associations, Synagogues, and Congregations*, 203–4.

67. Some evidence suggests that Jews actually prospered in the early empire. One example is the "Speech of Nicholas" in Josephus, *Antiquities* 16:31-57.

68. John M. G. Barclay, *Jews in the Mediterranean Diaspora from Alexander to Trajan (323 BCE–117 CE)* (Berkeley: University of California Press, 1996), 268–9.

69. Ibid.

70. On this matter, see S. R. F. Price, *Rituals and Power: The Roman Imperial Cult in Asia Minor* (Cambridge: Cambridge University Press, 1984).

71. See especially Scott, *Domination and the Arts of Resistance*, 1–16.

72. Yarbro Collins, *Combat Myth*, 114.

73. Ibid., 115–16.

74. Ibid., 189.

75. Ibid., 118.

76. Aune, *Revelation 6–16*, 688.

77. For more on the hidden-messiah motif, see Yarbro Collins, *Combat Myth*, 122.

78. The dating of the book of Revelation has long been a contentious issue among modern scholars. Three dates have been proposed: (1) the reign of Nero with empire-wide persecutions, (2a) the reign of Domitian with empire-wide persecutions, (2b) the reign of Domitian with sporadic

persecutions, and (3) the reign of Trajan with empire-wide persecutions. I here assume 2b, especially as argued by Adela Yarbro Collins, *Crisis and Catharsis: The Power of the Apocalypse* (Philadelphia: Westminster, 1984), 54–77. For similar arguments, see David A. de Silva, "The Social Setting of the Revelation of John: Conflicts Within, Fears Without," WTJ 54 (1992): 273–302; Leonard L. Thompson, *The Book of Revelation: Apocalypse and Empire* (New York: Oxford University Press, 1990), 197ff.; and Helmut Koester, *History and Literature of Early Christianity* (Introduction to the New Testament 2; New York: de Gruyter, 1980), 251ff.

79. Yarbro Collins, *Crisis and Catharsis*, 85–6.

80. Ibid., 87.

81. Michael Rostovtzeff, *The Social and Economic History of the Roman Empire* (Oxford: Clarendon, 1926), 111.

82. Yarbro Collins, *Crisis and Catharsis*, 101.

83. These sources are based on the analyses of Adela Yarbro Collins in *The Combat Myth*. See esp. pp. 101–55.

84. Reconstructed in Collins, *The Combat Myth*, 116.

85. Reconstructed in ibid., 137.

86. Reconstructed in ibid., 115.

87. Reconstructed in ibid., 116.

88. Yarbro Collins, *Crisis and Catharsis*, 143, argues that the form of the combat myth represented in Source II is directly from the Canaanite myth of Athtar, who attempted to dethrone Baal.

89. Ibid., 130.

90. Ibid., 131.

91. Ibid., 75.

92. Ibid., 131.

93. Ibid., 131.

94. See especially Revelation 13.

CHAPTER 2: SEVENTEENTH-CENTURY MEXICO

1. "Creole" in this context denotes Spaniards born on Mexican soil.

2. See Robert Choquette, Charles H. Lippy, and Stafford Poole, *Christianity Comes to the Americas: 1492–1776* (New York: Paragon, 1992), 4.

3. Ibid., 4.

4. Ibid., 6.

5. Ibid., 17.

6. These people are more accurately designated Northern African Berbers under the leadership of Syrian Muslim Arabs.

7. To label this entire period as the *reconquista* is inaccurate. Although the period of 718 to 1492 C.E. was a period of ongoing battles between Christian "Spaniards" under Muslim political control, the period also had significant moments of cooperation and interaction between Christians, Jews, and Muslims. For a detailed sketch of this historical period, see María Rosa Menocal, *Ornament of the World: How Muslims, Jews, and Christians Created a Culture of Tolerance in Medieval Spain* (New York: Little, Brown, 2002).

8. Choquette et al., *Christianity Comes to the Americas*, 3–4.

9. For a detailed discussion on the *patronato*, see ibid., 8–10.

10. Ibid., 12.

11. For a detailed study of this topic, see John Leddy Phelan, *The Millennial Kingdom of the Franciscans in the New World* (Berkeley: University of California Press, 1970).

12. Ibid., 14 (emphasis added).

13. In 1523, three Flemish Franciscans arrived in the Americas. In 1524, they were followed by twelve Spanish Franciscans who landed on the Eastern Coast of Veracruz, Mexico. According to Choquette et al., *Christianity Comes to the Americas*, 32, the number twelve was no coincidence and was highly symbolic of the Twelve Apostles. They made the long journey to Tenochtitlán by foot in tattered clothes and were greeted by the kneeling Cortés and conquistadors with kisses on their hands and the hems of their worn garments. The spectacle was witnessed by many of the inhabitants of Tenochtitlán and is sometimes labeled the beginning of the so-called spiritual conquest of Mexico.

14. Jacques Lafaye, *Quetzalcóatl and Guadalupe: The Formation of a Mexican National Consciousness, 1531–1813* (Chicago: University of Chicago Press, 1976), 32.

15. I argue later in this chapter that this recontextualization at the genesis of this Creole spirit would evolve into outright subversion in the seventeenth century.

16. Lafaye, *Quetzalcóatl and Guadalupe*, 32.

17. For more on Mendieta, see Phelan, *The Millennial Kingdom*, 11.

18. Ibid., 11–12.

19. Lafaye labels the anachronistic separation of church and state in this matter as "confusion"; it would be more appropriate to recognize these two categories as a unified order.

20. Choquette et al., *Christianity Comes to the Americas*, 18.

21. Phelan, *The Millennial Kingdom*, 21.

22. Ibid., 22.

23. Ibid., 22–23.

24. Lafaye, *Quetzalcóatl and Guadalupe*, 217–18.

25. Ibid., 218.

26. For the most comprehensive discussion on the issue of medieval apparitions in Spain, see William A. Christian Jr., *Apparitions in Late Medieval and Renaissance Spain* (Princeton: Princeton University Press, 1981).

27. Lafaye, *Quetzalcóatl and Guadalupe*, 219.

28. Codex 555, Madrid, Archico Histórico Nacional, fol. 5v., cited in Lafaye, *Quetzalcóatl and Guadalupe*, 220.

29. Lafaye, *Quetzalcóatl and Guadalupe*, 221.

30. Codex 555, Madrid, Archivo Histórico Nacional, fols. 6r–8r, cited in Lafaye, *Quetzalcóatl and Guadalupe*, 219.

31. P. Diego de Ecija, *Libro de la invención de Santa María de Guadalupe*, ed. Fr. A. Barrado Manzano, O.F.M. (Caceres, 1953), cited by Lafaye, *Quetzalcóatl and Guadalupe*, 219.

32. Lafaye, *Quetzalcóatl and Guadalupe*, 22.

33. See Choquette et al., *Christianity Comes to the Americas*, 26.

34. Ibid., 27.

35. Ibid., 29.

36. Ibid.

37. Ibid.

38. For a detailed discussion on Nahua (Mexica/Aztec) polytheism, see Miguel León Portilla, *Aztec Thought and Culture* (Norman: University of Oklahoma Press, 1990), 70. He argues that:

the popular religion of the Nahuas was not only polytheistic, it was also an amalgam of diverse regional gods. During the reign of the last king, Motecuhzoma, a great number of the gods of other peoples were freely assimilated by the popular religion. For the diversity of the assimilated gods, a special temple called *Coateocalli* (temple of many gods) was erected within the great Tenochtitlan, and, consequently, the number of deities that were worshipped increased day by day.

39. See Louis M. Burkhart, *Before Guadalupe: The Virgin Mary in Early Colonial Nahuatl Literature* (Austin: University of Texas Press, 2001), 2–3; and Luis Weckman, *La herencia medieval de Mexico* (Mexico City: Colegio de México, 1984), 1:199–207.

40. Burkhart, *Before Guadalupe*, 3.

41. Lafaye, *Quetzalcóatl and Guadalupe*, 226.

42. The first Dominicans arrived in 1526. They too arrived with the symbolic number of twelve missionaries. They were followed by the first Augustinians (1533) and the Jesuits (1572).

43. Choquette et al., *Christianity Comes to the Americas*, 32.

44. Robert Ricard, *The Spiritual Conquest of Mexico* (trans. Lesley Byrd Simpson; Berkeley: University of California Press, 1966).

45. For a detailed examination, see Stafford Poole, C.M., *Our Lady of Guadalupe: The Origins and Sources of a Mexican National Symbol, 1531–1797* (Tucson: University of Arizona Press, 1997), 59–61.

46. Ibid., 59 (emphasis added).

47. Miles Philips' account has been preserved in several works. This particular passage was taken from *Hakluyt's Voyages*, edited and translated by Richard Davis (Boston: Houghton Mifflin, 1981), 414, cited by Poole, *Our Lady of Guadalupe*, 69–70. Of note is the mention of the icon being a statue rather than the expected painting. It may be significant also that in 1566, seven years before the corsair transcribed his account, the *ermita* received a gift of a silver statue of Guadalupe from a patron named Juan de Villaseca.

48. Bernardino de Sahagún, *Florentine Codex: General History of the Things of New Spain*, trans. Arthur J. O. Anderson and Charles E. Dibble (Santa Fe, N.M.: School of American Research and University of Utah, 1958), 3:352.

49. Burkhart, *Before Guadalupe*, 1.

50. Choquette et al., *Christianity Comes to the Americas*, 41.

51. Lafaye, *Quetzalcóatl and Guadalupe*, 7.

52. Ibid., 8.

53. Ibid., 41.

54. Several traditions maintain that the soldier's name was Juan Rodríguez de Villafuente.

55. Various dates are attributed to the rediscovery of the statuette, including 1540, 1544, and 1555.

56. This paraphrase of the Remedios tradition is from Poole, *Our Lady of Guadalupe*, 24–5.

57. Lafaye, *Quetzalcóatl and Guadalupe*, 233–4.

58. The issue of the Virgin of Tepeyac being pregnant has long been debated. Proponents of this idea note the *cinta* (belt) worn high on her belly. In indigenous cultures, the *cinta* is worn by pregnant women.

59. Poole, *Our Lady of Guadalupe*, 100–1.

60. For more on the biography of Sánchez, see ibid., 101; and Timothy Matovina, "Guadalupe at Calvary: Patristic Theology in Miguel Sánchez's *Imagen de la Virgen María* (1648)," TS 64 (2003): 796–7.

61. Poole, *Our Lady of Guadalupe*, 101.

62. Matovina, "Guadalupe at Calvary," 796–7.

63. For more on the contents of the book, see Poole, *Our Lady of Guadalupe*, 101; and Jean-Pierre Ruiz, "The Bible and U.S. Hispanic American Theological Discourse: Lessons from a Non-Innocent History," in *From the Heart of Our People: Latino/a Explorations in Catholic Systematic Theology*, ed. Orlando O. Espín and Miguel H. Díaz (Maryknoll: Orbis, 1999), 106.

64. Matovina, "Guadalupe at Calvary," 800.

65. Lafaye, *Quetzalcóatl and Guadalupe*, 250.

66. Sánchez, Miguel. "Imagen de la Virgen María Madre de Dios de Guadalupe (1648)." *Testimonios históricos guadalupanos*. Ed. By Ernesto de la Torre Villar and Ramiro Navarro de Anda. México, D. F.: Fondo de Cultura Economica (1982): 152–281.

67. Ibid., 231.

68. Ibid., 195.

69. Ibid., 219.

70. Poole, *Our Lady of Guadalupe*, 106–7.

71. Ibid., 109.

72. Ibid.

73. Matovina, "Guadalupe at Calvary," 800.

74. Lafaye, *Qutzalcóatl and Guadalupe*, 250.

75. Scott, *Domination and the Arts of Resistance*, xii.

76. Choquette et al., *Christianity Comes to the Americas*, 46.

77. Burkhart, *Before Guadalupe*, 2.

78. Matovina, "Guadalupe at Calvary," 797 (emphasis added).

79. Ruiz, "The Bible and U.S. Hispanic American Theological Discourse," 106–7 (emphasis added).

80. Poole, *Our Lady of Guadalupe*, 107.

81. De la Vega's *Huei tlamahuiçoltica* is the topic of pages 76–82.

82. Sánchez, *Imagen*, translated in Poole, *Our Lady of Guadalupe*, 102. The attestation of a surviving indigenous, oral tradition is affected positively by the results of the now-famous Capitular Inquiry of 1665–1666.

83. The exact dates of publication for these two works are: *Imagen*, July 2, 1648, and the *Huei tlamahuiçoltica*, January 9, 1649.

84. The term *racionero* was given to a religious who performed liturgical duties with no administrative responsibilities in a given parish. A *medio* (half) *racionero* received half of the usual salary paid to "full" *racioneros*.

85. Poole, *Our Lady of Guadalupe*, 110.

86. Ibid., 111.

87. There has been much discussion as to the authorship of all or portions of the *Huei tlamahuiçoltica*. For my purpose, authorship issues are not primary concerns. What is relevant is that this text was first published in totality under the name of Luis Laso de la Vega, letter contributor to the *Imagen*, shortly after its production. For a detailed discussion on authorship theories, see Poole, *Our Lady of Guadalupe*, 112. In short, Poole concludes, "The book is clearly a compilation of diverse elements, dating from different periods and written in varying styles" (111).

88. Barbara Harlow, *Resistance Literature* (New York: Methuen, 1987), xviii.

89. From Stafford Poole C. M., Lisa Sousa and James Lockhart, trans. and eds., *The Story of Guadalupe: Luis Laso de la Vega's Huei tlamahuiçoltica, 1649* (Palo Alto, Calif.: Stanford University Press, 1998), 2.

90. Again, it must be emphasized that the *Huei tlamahuiçoltica* was only initially unsuccessful in persuading the Mexica toward Guadalupan devotion (the *Imagen* had no effect on them). It was ultimately the *Huei tlamahuiçoltica* that captured the imaginations of the Mexica (from the eighteenth century on) and continues to capture the imagination of contemporary Mexicans and Chicanas/os (esp. the *Nican mopohua*).

91. Poole, Sousa, and Lockhart, trans. and eds., *The Story of Guadalupe*, 55.

92. Ibid., 3. See also Ruiz, "The Bible and U.S. Hispanic American Theological Discourse," 109.

93. I do not contend that Laso de la Vega indigenizes the *Imagen*, only that he indigenizes the Creole tradition behind the *Imagen*. According to Poole, at least one part of Laso de la Vega's work, the *Nican mopohua*, "does not appear to be directly dependent on Sánchez's work." Poole, *Our Lady of Guadalupe*, 112.

94. Ibid., 119 and 126.

95. Ruiz, "The Bible and U.S. Hispanic American Theological Discourse," 111.

96. Poole, Sousa and Lockhart, trans. and eds, *The Story of Guadalupe*, 119.

97. Ibid., 121.

98. Poole, *Our Lady of Guadalupe*, 120.

99. Ibid., 121.

100. Ruiz, "The Bible and U.S. Hispanic American Theological Discourse," 106.

CHAPTER 3: TODAY

1. *El Plan* was a derivative of the First National Chicano Youth Liberation Congress, held in Denver in 1969. I discuss *El Plan* in reference to Manifest Destiny later in this chapter.

2. Richard T. Hughes, *Myths America Lives By* (Chicago: University of Illinois Press, 2003), 19.

3. Ibid., 106.

4. Ibid.

5. Louis O'Sullivan; cited by Alan Brinkley, *American History: A Survey* (2 vols.; 9th ed.; New York: McGraw-Hill, 1995) (emphasis added).

6. Robert W. Johannsen, "Introduction," in *Manifest Destiny and Empire: American Antebellum Expansionism,* ed. Sam W. Haynes and Christopher Morris (College Station: Texas A&M Press, 1997), 10.

7. Ibid., 3.

8. Ibid., 15.

9. Frederick Merk, *Manifest Destiny and Mission in American History: A Reinterpretation* (New York: Alfred A. Knopf, 1963), 24-26.

10. O'Sullivan, *Democtratic Review,* 243-48; cited in ibid., 24.

11. Burton L. Mack, *A Myth of Innocence: Mark and Christian Origins* (Philadelphia: Fortress Press, 1988), 369.

12. Ibid., 373.

13. Ibid., 370.

14. Rodolfo Acuña, *Occupied America: A History of Chicanos* (New York: Harper & Row, 1988), 50.

15. Ray A. Billington and James B. Hedges, *Westward Expansion: A History of the American Frontier* (New York: Macmillan, 1949), 572.

16. Acuña, *Occupied America,* 52.

17. Albert K. Weinberg, *Manifest Destiny: A Study of Nationalist Expansion in American History* (Baltimore: John Hopkins University Press, 1935), 169.

18. James M. McCaffrey, *Army of Manifest Destiny: The American Soldier in the Mexican War: 1846–1848* (New York: New York University Press, 1992), 79.

19. *United States Democratic Review* 41 (1858).

20. Walt Whitman, *The Gathering Forces* (New York: Putnam's Sons, 1920), 1:240.

21. William Starr Meyers, ed., *The Mexican War Diary of General B. Chellan* (Princeton: Princeton University Press, 1917), 1:161–2.

22. Ibid., 109–10.

23. Samuel E. Chamberlain, *My Confessions* (New York: Harper & Row, 1956), 87–8 (emphasis added).

24. Acuña, *Occupied America,* 55.

25. For a succinct analysis of the Treaty of Guadalupe Hidalgo, see ibid., 56–9.

26. The U.S. Senate Statement of Protocol; cited by Acuña, *Occupied America*, 57.

27. Acuña, *Occupied America*, 57.

28. Armando B. Rendón, *Chicano Manifesto* (New York: Collier, 1970), 75–8; cited by Acuña, *Occupied America*, 57.

29. Richard Griswold del Castillo, *The Treaty of Guadalupe Hidalgo: A Legacy of Conflict* (Norman: University of Oklahoma Press, 1990), 131–2.

30. Rodolfo Acuña, *Anything but Mexican: Chicanos in Contemporary Los Angeles* (New York: Verso, 1996), 9.

31. Ibid.

32. See Matt S. Meier and Feliciano Rivera, *Dictionary of Mexican American History* (Westport, Conn.: Greenwood, 1981), 83–4.

33. Alicia Gaspar de Alba, *Chicano Art: Inside/outside the Master's House: Cultural Politics and the CARA Exhibition* (Austin: University of Texas Press, 1998), 42.

34. Rafael Pérez-Torres, "Reconfiguring Aztlán," in *The Chicano Studies Reader: An Anthology of Aztlán 1970–2000*, ed. Eric R. Avila et al. (Los Angeles: Chicano Studies Research Center, 2001), 216.

35. Acuña, *Occupied America*, 411.

36. Américo Paredes, *"With His Pistol in His Hand": A Border Ballad and Its Hero* (Austin: University of Texas Press, 1958), 15–16. For a discussion of these stereotypes, see Gaspar de Alba, *Chicano Art*, 65.

37. For a detailed discussion of these issues, see Shifra M. Goldman and Tomas Ybarra-Frausto, "The Political and Social Contexts in Chicano Art," in *CARA: Chicano Art: Resistance and Affirmation,* ed. Richard Griswold del Castillo, Teresa McKenna, and Yvonne Yarbro-Bejarano (Los Angeles: Wright Art Gallery, UCLA, 1991), 83.

38. Ibid.

39. Ibid., 139.

40. Ibid.

41. For a full discussion of Hidalgo y Costilla, see Enrique Krauze, *Mexico: A Biography of Power, 1810–1996* (New York: Harper, 1998), 91–101.

42. See Griswold del Castillo, *The Treaty of Guadalupe Hidalgo*, 132.

43. Ibid., 134.

44. Ibid., 139, 153.

45. Rendón, *Chicano Manifesto*, 81.

46. Ibid., 84–5.

47. Griswold del Castillo, *The Treaty of Guadalupe Hidalgo*, 139 (emphasis added).

48. The Brown Berets were founded in 1967 by David Sánchez, a former chairman of the Los Angeles Mayor's Youth Council. Eventually, the Berets claimed five thousand members nationwide. The goal of the Berets was to fulfill the ideals articulated in *El Plan Espiritual de Aztlan*, namely, to control or at least have a voice in the policies that affected Chicanos: schools, police, welfare offices, and the immigration service. As an action-oriented militant organization, the Berets participated in and helped organize most of the major landmark episodes of the Chicano movement.

49. Griswold del Castillo, *The Treaty of Guadalupe Hidalgo*, 140, 142, 144.

50. Armando Navarro, *Mexicano Political Experience in Occupied Aztlán: Struggles and Change* (New York: Alta Mira, 2005), 337.

51. Ibid.

52. Goldman and Ybarra-Frausto, "Political and Social Contexts," 84.

53. Cited by Navarro, *Mexicano Political Experience*, 337–8 (emphasis added).

54. Rafael Pérez-Torres, "Reconfiguring Aztlán," in *The Chicano Studies Reader: An Anthology of Aztlán 1970–2000*, ed. Eric R. Avila et al. (Los Angeles: Chicano Studies Research Center, 2001), 213.

55. An analysis of Chicana/o rhetoric of resistance reveals an explicit connection to the ancient Aztecs—one of their basic and perhaps even uncritical assumptions.

56. Pérez-Torres, "Reconfiguring Aztlán," 214.

57. *La raza* is an ethnocentric term of ethnic pride employed by *el Movimiento* (The Chicana/o Movement) and is simply translated as "the Race."

58. Clifford Geertz, "Art as a Cultural System," MLN 91 (1976): 1473–99.

59. Tomas Ybarra-Frausto, "Arte Chicano: Images of a Community," in *Signs from the Heart: California Chicano Murals*, ed. Eva Sperling Cockcroft and Holly Barnet-Sánchez (Albuquerque: University of New Mexico Press, 1993), 55.

60. Eva Sperling Cockcroft and Holly Barnet-Sánchez, "Introduction," in *Signs from the Heart*, 5.

61. Shifra M. Goldman, "How, Why, Where, and When It All Happened: Chicano Murals of California," in Cockcroft and Barnet-Sánchez, *Signs from the Heart*, 28.

62. F. Arturo Rosales, *Chicano: The History of the Mexican American Civil Rights Movement* (Houston: Arte Público, 1996), 256.

63. Shifra M. Goldman, "Mexican Muralism: Its Social-Educative Roles in Latin America and the United States," in *The Chicano Studies Reader: An Anthology of Aztlán 1970–2000*, ed. Eric R. Avila et al. (Los Angeles: Chicano Studies Research Center Publications, 2001), 281–2.

64. Cockcroft and Barnet-Sánchez, "Introduction," 9–10.

65. Desmond Rochfort, *Mexican Muralists: Orozco, Rivera, Siqueiros* (San Francisco: Chronicle, 1993), 11.

66. Goldman and Ybarra-Frausto, "Political and Social Contexts," 85. For a discussion of the UFW's employment of the red, black, and white thunderbird flag, see Jacques E. Levy, *César Chávez: Autobiography of La Causa* (New York: Norton, 1975), chap. 4. In this chapter (at p. 173), Chávez himself gives a brief summation of the choice of the symbol:

> We needed an emblem for the Union, a flag that people could see. Many ideas were suggested, but we wanted something that the people could make themselves, and something that had some impact. We didn't want a tractor or a crossed shovel and a hoe or a guy with a hoe and pruning shears. I liked the Mexican eagle with a snake in its mouth, but it was too hard to draw.

67. Quoted by Andrés G. Guerrero, *A Chicano Theology* (Maryknoll: Orbis, 1987), 105–6.

68. This is especially the case with Luis Laso de la Vega's composition of the myth (1649), and it is this particular rendition of the myth that continues to captivate the imaginations of both its religiously and politically motivated appropriators.

69. Her significations are much greater than simply that of territorial proprietorship, but this is appears to be at least one motif that the Chicana/o movement drew from extensively.

70. See p. 84, above.

71. The Chicana/o equivalent of "Uncle Tom."

CONCLUSION

1. Homi K. Bhabha, *The Location of Culture* (New York: Routledge, 1994), 1.

2. Nick Crossley, *Key Concepts in Critical Social Theory* (London: Sage, 2005), 129.

3. For more on the hybrid agent as occupant of this intercultural location, see Franz Fannon, *Black Skins, White Masks* (New York: Grove, 1991).

4. See Bill Ashcroft, Gareth Griffiths, and Helen Tiffin, eds., *The Post-Colonial Studies Reader* (London: Routledge, 1995), 12–13.

5. Ibid., 139. The colonizers themselves do not seek an exact replica from their colonial subjects; this would be altogether much too threatening a situation. Rather, what the colonizers seek is a "reformed, recognizable Other, as a subject of difference that is almost the same but not quite." On this issue, see Bhabha, *The Location of Culture*, 86.

6. Ashcroft et al., eds., *Post-Colonial Studies Reader*, 139.

7. James C. Scott, *Domination and the Arts of Resistance: Hidden Transcripts* (New Haven: Yale University Press, 1990), xii.

8. Samuel Weber, "The sideshow, or: remarks on a canny moment," *Modern Language Notes*, vol. 88, no. 6 (1973), 112.

9. James C. Scott, *Weapons of the Weak: Everyday Forms of Peasant Resistance* (New Haven: Yale University Press, 1985), xvii.

10. See above, introduction, n. 6.

11. Bhabha, *The Location of Culture*, 86.

12. Ashcroft et al., eds., *Post-Colonial Studies Reader*, 140–1.

13. Ibid., 13, 139, 140, 141.

14. Ibid., 141 (emphasis added).

15. Crossley, *Key Concepts*, 130.

16. Andrew Smith, "Migrancy, Hybridity, and Postcolonial Literary Studies," in *The Cambridge Companion to Postcolonial Literary Studies*, ed. Neil Lazarus (Cambridge: Cambridge University Press, 2004), 241–61 (emphasis added).

17. Annie E. Coombes, "The Recalcitrant Object: Cultural Contact and the Question of Hybridity," in *Colonial Discourse/Postcolonial Theory*, ed. Francis Barker, Peter Hulme, and Margaret Iverson (Manchester: Manchester University Press, 1994), 91.

18. Fernando F. Segovia, "Interpreting Beyond Borders: Postcolonial Studies and Diasporic Studies in Biblical Criticism," in *Interpreting Beyond Borders*, ed. Segovia (The Bible and Colonialism 3; Sheffield: Sheffield Academic, 2000), 13–14.

19. Ibid.

20. See above, introduction, n. 8.

21. Ashcroft et al., eds. *Post-Colonial Studies Reader*, 141.

22. Bhabha, *The Location of Culture*, 86.

23. Burton L. Mack, *A Myth of Innocence: Mark and Christian Origins* (Philadelphia: Fortress Press, 1988), 373.

24. Paulo Freire, *Pedagogy of the Oppressed* (New York: Continuum, 2003); see esp. pp. 45–50. In this section, Freire makes the following observation:

> Who are better prepared than the oppressed to understand the terrible significance of an oppressive society? Who suffer the effects of oppression more than the oppressed? Who can better understand the necessity of liberation? They will not gain this liberation by chance but through the praxis of their quest for it, through their necessity to fight for it.

25. Vincent L. Wimbush, "Reading Darkness, Reading Scripture," in *African Americans and the Bible: Sacred Texts and Social Textures*, ed. Wimbush (New York: Continuum, 2000), 9.

26. Fernando F. Segovia, "Reading the Bible Ideologically: Socioeconomic Criticism," in *To Each Its Own Meaning: An Introduction to Biblical Criticisms and Their Applications*, ed. Steven L. McKenzie and Stephen R. Haynes (rev. ed.; Louisville: Westminster John Knox, 1999), 29 (emphasis added).

27. Wimbush, "Reading Darkness," 9.

28. Ibid.

29. Ibid., 19.

30. Segovia, "Reading the Bible Ideologically," 31–2.

31. Wimbush, "Reading Darkness," 12.

32. Jean Pierre Ruiz, "Taking a Stand on the Seashore: A Postcolonial Exploration of Revelation 13," in *Reading the Book of Revelation: A Resource for Students*, ed. David L. Barr (Atlanta: Society of Biblical Literature, 2003), 124.

33. Ibid., 124–5.

34. Wimbush, "Reading Darkness," 14.

APPENDIX 1

1. James Lockhart argues that the *Nican mopohua* may have been written anywhere between 1550 and 1560, or even later (*The Nahuas After the Conquest: A Social and Cultural History of the Indians of Central Mexico, Sixteenth through Eighteenth Centuries* [Stanford, Calif.: Stanford University Press, 1992], 250).

APPENDIX 2

1. *Aztlán* is a multivalent term, referring at once to northern lands from which the Aztecs migrated into the Valley of Mexico and to the land taken by the United States under the aegis of "manifest destiny" following the U.S.-Mexican War (present day Arizona, New Mexico, and parts of Texas and California). The term also evokes a utopian land where a future Chicana/o nation will be built; see above, p. 103.

2. *Gabacho*: a derogatory term for a non-Spanish-speaking white person in the Chicano community.

3. *Mestizo*: a person of mixed ethnic ancestry, especially of mixed European and Native American ancestry.

4. *Pueblo*: people.

5. *Por La Raza todo. Fuera de La Raza nada.* "For the [Mexican] race, everything. Outside the race, nothing."

6. *Campos*: agricultural fields.

7. *Carnalismo*: a slang term referring to a form of Chicano/a or Mexican solidarity.

BIBLIOGRAPHY

THE BOOK OF REVELATION, ANCIENT STUDIES, AND PRIMARY SOURCES

Alter, Robert, and Frank Kermode, eds. *The Literary Guide to the Bible*. Cambridge, Mass.: Harvard University Press, 1987.

Apollodorus. *Apollodorus, The Library*. Translated by James G. Frazer. LCL. Cambridge, Mass.: Harvard University Press, 1961.

Augustus Caesar. "Res Gestae Divi Augusti." In *The New Testament Background: Writings from Ancient Greece and the Roman Empire That Illuminate Christian Origins*. Edited by C. K Barrett. San Francisco: Harper San Francisco, 1989.

Aune, David E. "The Influence of the Roman Imperial Court Setting Ceremonial on the Apocalypse of John." *BR* 28 (1983): 5–26.

———. *Revelation*. WBC. Three volumes. *Revelation 1–5*. Dallas: Word, 1997. *Revelation 6–16*. Nashville: Thomas Nelson, 1998. *Revelation 17–20*. Nashville: Thomas Nelson, 1998.

———. "The Social Matrix of the Apocalypse of John." *BR* 26 (1981): 16–32.

Backus, Irena Dorata. *Reformation Readings of the Apocalypse: Geneva, Zurich, Wittenberg*. Oxford: Oxford University Press, 2000.

Balch, David A. "Hellenization/Acculturation in 1 Peter." Pages 70–101 in *Perspectives on First Peter*. Macon, Ga.: Mercer University Press, 1986.

———. *Let Wives Be Submissive: The Domestic Code in 1 Peter*. SBLMS 26. Chico, Calif.: Scholars, 1981.

———. "'A Woman Clothed with the Sun' and the 'Great Red Dragon' Seeking to 'Devour Her Child' (Rev. 12:1, 4) in Roman Domestic Art." Unpublished manuscript.

Barclay, John M. G. *Jews in the Mediterranean Diaspora from Alexander to Trajan (323 BCE–117 CE)*. Berkeley: University of California Press, 1996.

Bell, Albert. "The Date of the Apocalypse: The Evidence of Some Roman Historians Reconsidered." *NTS* 25 (1978): 93–102.

Biguzzi, G. "John on Patmos and the 'Persecution' in the Apocalypse." *Estudios Biblicos* 56 (1998): 201–20.

Bissonette, G. "The Twelfth Chapter of the Apocalypse and Our Lady's Assumption." *Marian Studies* 2 (1951): 170–92.

Böcher, O. "Johanneisches in der Apokalypse der Johannes." *NTS* 27 (1981): 310–21.

Boesak, Allan. *Comfort and Protest: The Apocalypse from a South African Perspective*. Philadelphia: Westminster, 1987.

Boring, Eugene M. *Revelation*. Nashville: John Knox, 1989.

Bousset, Wilhelm. *Die Offenbarung Johannis*. KEK 16. 6th ed. Göttingen: Vandenhoeck & Ruprecht, 1906.

Bowerstock, Glen W. *Augustus and the Greek World*. Oxford: Clarendon, 1965.

Bradley, K. R. *Slaves and Masters in the Roman Empire: A Study in Social Control*. New York: Oxford University Press, 1987.

Brasher, B. E. "From Revelation to the X-Files: An Autopsy of Millennialism in American Popular Culture." *Semeia* 82 (1998): 281–95.

Braun, F. M. "La Femme Vetue de Soliel." *RThom* 35 (1955): 639–69.

Brown, Raymond E., et al., eds. *The Jerome Biblical Commentary*. Englewood Cliffs, N.J.: Prentice-Hall, 1968.

Bruns, J. E. "The Contrasted Women of Apocalypse 12 and 17." *CBQ* 26 (1964): 459–63.

Caird, G. B. *A Commentary on the Revelation of St. John the Divine*. Black's New Testament Commentaries. London: Black, 1966.

Callimachus. "Hymn to Apollo and Hymn to Delos." In *Callimachus, Lycophron, Aratus*. Translated by A. W. Mair. LCL. Cambridge, Mass.: Harvard University Press, 1960.

Cambier, Jules, and Lucien Cerfaux. *L'Apocalypse de Saint Jean lue aux Chretiens*. Paris: Cerf, 1964.

Charlesworth, James, ed. *The Messiah: Developments in Earliest Judaism and Christianity*. Minneapolis: Fortress Press, 1992.

Chevalier, Jacques M. *A Postmodern Revelation: Signs of Astrology and the Apocalypse.* Toronto: University of Toronto Press, 1997.

Collins, John J. "Apocalypse and Apocalypticism (Early Jewish Apocalypticism)." Pages 282–8 in *ABD* 1. Edited by David N. Freeman. New York: Doubleday, 1992.

——. *The Apocalyptic Imagination: An Introduction to the Jewish Matrix of Christianity.* New York: Crossroad, 1992.

——, ed. *The Encyclopedia of Apocalypticism: The Origins of Apocalypticism in Judaism and Christianity.* New York: Continuum, 2000.

——. "Introduction: Towards the Morphology of a Genre." *Semeia* 14 (1979): 1–20.

——. *The Scepter and the Star: The Messiahs of the Dead Sea Scrolls and Other Ancient Literature.* New York: Doubleday, 1995.

Comaroff, Jean, and John Comaroff. *Of Revelation and Revolution: Christianity, Colonialism and Consciousness in South Africa.* Chicago: University of Chicago Press, 1991.

Conte, Gian Biagio. *The Rhetoric of Imitation: Genre and Poetic Memory in Virgil and Other Latin Poets.* Ithaca, N.Y.: Cornell University Press, 1986.

Cukrowski, K. "The Influence on the Emperor Cult on the Book of Revelation." *RQ* 45 (2003): 51–64.

Cullman, Oscar. *Christology of the New Testament.* London: SCM, 1959.

de Silva, David A. "Honor Discourse and the Rhetorical Strategy of the Apocalypse of John." *JSNT* 71 (1998): 79–110.

——. "The Social Setting of the Revelation of John: Conflicts Within, Fears Without." *WTJ* 54 (1992): 273–302.

Dietrich, Albrecht. *Abraxas: Studien zur Reliogiongeschicte des spätern Altertums.* Leipzig: Teubner, 1923.

Downing, F. G. "Pliny's Persecution of Christians: Revelation and 1 Peter." *JSNT* 34 (1988): 105–23.

Duff, P. B. *Who Rides the Beast? Prophetic Rivalry and the Rhetoric of Crisis in the Churches of the Apocalypse.* New York: Oxford University Press, 2001.

Duling, Dennis, and Norman Perrin. *The New Testament: Proclamation and Parenesis, Myth and History.* New York: Harcourt Brace, 1993.

Dunn, James D. G. *Jesus Remembered*. Grand Rapids: Eerdmans, 2003.

Elliot, John A. *A Home for the Homeless: A Social-Scientific Criticism of 1 Peter, Its Situation and Strategy*. 2nd ed. Minneapolis: Fortress Press, 1990.

Euripides. "Iphegenia in Taurus." In *Euripides*. Translated by A. S. Way. LCL 2. New York: Macmillan, 1912.

Faley, Roland. *Apocalypse Then and Now: A Companion to the Book of Revelation*. Mahwah, N.J.: Paulist, 1999.

Fontenrose, Joseph. *Python: A Study of the Delphic Myth and Its Origins*. Berkeley: University of California Press, 1959.

Forsyth, Neil. *The Old Enemy: Satan and the Combat Myth*. Princeton: Princeton University Press, 1987.

Foulkes, Ricardo. *El Apocalipsis de San Juan*. Buenos Aires: Nueva Creació, 1989.

Friesen, Steven J. *Imperial Cults and the Apocalypse of John: Reading Revelation in the Ruins*. Oxford: Oxford University Press, 2001.

———. *Twice Neokoros: Ephesus, Asia, and the Cult of the Flavian Imperial Family*. RGRW 116. Leiden: Brill, 1993.

Fuller, Reginald. *A New Catholic Commentary on Holy Scripture*. London: Nelson, 1975.

Gager, J. G. *Kingdom and Community: The Social World of Early Christianity*. New York: Prentice-Hall, 1975.

Galinsky, Karl. *Augustan Culture: An Interpretive Introduction*. Princeton: Princeton University Press, 1996.

Garrett, Susan. "Revelation." Pages 469–74 in *The Women's Bible Commentary*. Edited by Carol Newsom and Sharon Ringe. Louisville: Westminster John Knox, 1998.

Gentry, K. L. *Before Jerusalem Fell: The Dating of the Book of Revelation*. Tyler, Tex.: Institute for Christian Economics, 1989.

Gibbs, Nancy. "Apocalypse Now." *Time*, July 1, 2002, pp. 40-48.

González, Catherine Gunzalus, and Justo González. *Revelation*. Louisville: Westminster John Knox, 1997.

Gradel, L. *Emperor Worship and Roman Religion*. Oxford: Oxford University Press, 2002.

Grant, Mary, ed. and trans. *The Myths of Hyginus*. Lawrence: University of Kansas Press, 1960.

Gunkel, Hermann. *Schöpfung und chaos in Urzeit und Endzeit: Eine religiongeschictliche Unterschung über Gen. 1 und Ap. Joh. 12.* Göttingen: Vandenhoeck & Ruprecht, 1895.

Hanson, Paul D. *The Dawn of Apocalyptic.* Philadelphia: Fortress Press, 1975.

Harland, Philip A. *Associations, Synagogues, and Congregations: Claiming a Place in Ancient Mediterranean Society.* Philadelphia: Fortress Press, 2003.

———. "Honoring the Emperor or Assailing the Beast: Participation in Civic Life among the Associations in Asia Minor and the Apocalypse of John." *JSNT* 77 (2000): 99–121.

Harrison, E. *Studies in Theogonis.* Cambridge: Cambridge University Press, 1902.

Hedrick, W. K. "The Sources and Use of Imagery in Apocalypse 12." Diss., Graduate Theological Union, Berkeley, 1970.

Hellholm, David. "The Problem of the Apocalyptic Genre and the Apocalypse of John." Pages 157–98 in *Society of Biblical Literature 1982 Seminar Papers* (1982).

Hemer, C. J. *The Letters to the Seven Churches of Asia and Their Local Settings.* JSNTSup 11. Sheffield: JSOT, 1986.

Herodotus. *Herodotus.* Translated by A. D. Godley. LCL 1. New York: Putnam's Sons, 1921.

Hesiod. *The Homeric Hymns.* Translated by Hugh G. Evelyn-White. LCL. New York: Macmillan, 1914.

Horsley, Richard A. *Jesus and Empire: The Kingdom of God and the New World Disorder.* Minneapolis: Fortress Press, 2002.

———. "Messianic Figures and Movements in First-Century Palestine." Pages 276–95 in *The Messiah: Developments in Earliest Judaism and Christianity.* Edited by James Charlesworth. Minneapolis: Fortress Press, 1992.

———. *Paul and Empire: Religion and Power in Roman Imperial Society.* Harrisburg, Pa.: Trinity Press International, 1997.

Hort, F. J. A. *The Apocalypse of Saint John: The Greek Text with Introduction.* London: Macmillan, 1908.

Howard-Brook, W., and A. Gwyther. *Unveiling Empire: Reading Revelation Then and Now.* Maryknoll: Orbis, 1999.

Hunt, Stephen, ed. *Christian Millenarianism from the Early Church to Waco.* Bloomington: Indiana University Press, 2001.

Jackson, Rosemary. *Fantasy: The Literature of Subversion.* New York: Methuen, 1981.

Kassing, Altfrid T. *Die Kirche und Maria: Ihr Verhältnis im 12.* Kapitel der Apokalypse. Düsseldorf: Patmos, 1958.

Koester, Helmut. *History and Literature of Early Christianity.* Vol. 2. New York: de Gruyter, 1980.

———, ed. *Pergamon, Citadel of the Gods: Archaeological Record, Literary Description, and Religious Development.* Harrisburg, Pa.: Trinity Press International, 1998.

Krabel, A. T. "Judaism in Western Asia Minor under the Roman Empire, with a Preliminary Study of the Jewish Community at Sardis, Lydia." Diss., Harvard University, 1968.

Kraybill, Nelson. *Imperial Cult and Commerce in John's Apocalypse.* Sheffield: Sheffield Academic, 1996.

Kümmel, W. George. *Introduction to the New Testament.* London: SCM, 1970.

LeFrois, B. J. "The Mary-Church Relationship in the Apocalypse." *Marian Studies* 9 (1958): 79–106.

———. *The Woman Clothed with the Sun (Ap. 12), Individual or Collective?* Rome: Orbis Catholicus, 1954.

Leon, Harry J. *The Jews of Ancient Rome.* Updated ed. Peabody, Mass.: Hendrickson, 1995.

Lewis, James R., ed. *From the Ashes: Making Sense of Waco.* Lanham: Rowman & Littlefield, 1994.

Lightfoot, J. B. *Biblical Essays.* New York: Macmillan, 1893.

Lilje, Hans. *The Last Book of the Bible.* Philadelphia: Muhlenberg, 1957.

Lohmeyer, Ernst. *Die Offenbarung des Johannes.* HNT 16. Tübingen: Mohr (Siebeck), 1926.

Lucian. "Dialogues of the Sea Gods." In *Lucian.* Translated by M. D. Macleod. LCL 7. Cambridge, Mass.: Harvard University Press, 1961.

MacDonald, Dennis R. *The Homeric Epics and the Gospel of Mark.* New Haven: Yale University Press, 2000.

MacDonald, Margaret Y. *A Socio-historic Study of Institutionalization in the Pauline and Deutero-Pauline Writings.* SNTSMS 60. Cambridge: Cambridge University Press, 1988.

Mack, Burton L. *A Myth of Innocence: Mark and Christian Origins.* Philadelphia: Fortress Press, 1988.

Maier, Harry O. *Apocalypse Recalled: The Book of Revelation after Christendom.* Minneapolis: Fortress Press, 2002.

———. *The Social Setting of the Ministry as Reflected in the Writings of Hermas, Clement, and Ignatius.* Waterloo, Ontario: Wilfred Laurier University Press, 1991.

Malina, Bruce J., and John J. Pilch. *Social-Science Commentary on the Book of Revelation.* Minneapolis: Fortress Press, 2000.

Mann, Michael. *The Sources of Social Power.* 2 vols. New York: Cambridge University Press, 1986.

Marthaler, Bernard L., et al., eds. *The New Catholic Encyclopedia.* 12 vols. New York: Thomson Gale, 2003.

Mattern, S. P. *Rome and the Enemy: Imperial Strategy in the Principate.* Berkeley: University of California Press, 1999.

McHugh, John. *The Mother of Jesus in the New Testament.* Garden City, N.Y.: Doubleday, 1975.

McMullen, Ramsay. *Enemies of the Roman Order: Treason, Unrest, and Alienation in the Empire.* Cambridge, Mass.: Harvard University Press, 1966.

Meeks, Wayne. *The First Urban Christians: The Social World of the Apostle Paul.* New Haven: Yale University Press, 1983.

Metzger, Bruce M. *Breaking the Code: Understanding the Book of Revelation.* Nashville: Abingdon, 1993.

Meyers, Ched. *Binding the Strong Man: A Political Reading of Mark's Story of Jesus.* Maryknoll: Orbis, 1995.

Michael, Jacob. "Who Is the Woman of Revelation 12? A Study of the Twelfth Chapter of the Apocalypse." www.cathinsight.com /apologetics/womanrev12.htm.

Miller, Merrill P. "The Problems of the Origins of a Messianic Jesus." Pages 301–35 in *Redescribing Christian Origins.* Edited by Ron Cameron and Merrill P. Miller. Atlanta: Society of Biblical Literature, 2004.

Mounce, Robert H. *The Book of Revelation*. Grand Rapids: Eerdmans, 1977.

Müeller, U. B. "Lieterarische und formgeschitliche Bestimmung der Apokalypse des Johannes al seinen Zeugnis früchristlicher Apokalyptik." Pages 599–620 in *International Colloquium on Apocalypticism*. Edited by David Hellholm. Tübingen: Mohr (Siebeck), 1983.

Murphy, F. J. *Fallen Is Babylon: The Revelation of John*. Harrisburg, Pa.: Trinity Press International, 1998.

Murphy, R. E. "An Allusion to Mary in the Apocalypse 12." *TS* 10 (1949): 565–73.

Neusner, Jacob, et al. *Judaism and Their Messiahs at the Turn of the Christian Century*. New York: Cambridge University Press, 1987.

Pausanias. *Pausanias, Description of Greece*. Translated by W. H. S. Jones. LCL. Cambridge, Mass.: Harvard University Press, 1964.

Perkins, Judith. *The Suffering Self: Pain and Narrative Representation in the Early Christian Era*. New York: Routledge, 1995.

Pilch, John. *What Are They Saying about the Book of Revelation?* New York: Paulist, 1978.

Pindar. *The Odes of Pindar*. Translated by John Sandys. LCL. Cambridge, Mass.: Harvard University Press, 1961.

Pippin, Tina. *Apocalyptic Bodies: The Biblical End of the World in Text and Image*. New York: Routledge, 1999.

———. *Death and Desire: The Rhetoric of Gender in the Apocalypse of John*. Philadelphia: Westminster John Knox, 1992.

Plutarch. "On Isis and Osiris." In *Moralia*. Translated by F. C. Babbitt. LCL 5. Cambridge, Mass.: Harvard University Press, 1962.

———. "On the Obsolescence of Oracles." In *Moralia*. Translated by F. C. Babbitt. LCL 5. Cambridge, Mass.: Harvard University Press, 1962.

Price, S. R. F. *Rituals and Power: The Roman Imperial Cult in Asia Minor*. Cambridge: Cambridge University Press, 1984.

Pringent, Pierre. *Apocalypse 12: Histoire de l'exégèse*. Tübingen: Mohr (Siebeck), 1959.

Ramsey, Michael. *Interpreting the Book of Revelation*. Grand Rapids: Baker, 1992.

Rhoads, David, ed. *From Every People and Nation: The Book of Revelation in Intercultural Perspective*. Minneapolis: Fortress Press, 2005.

Richard, Pablo. *Apocalypse: A People's Commentary on the Book of Revelation.* Maryknoll: Orbis, 1995.

Robinson, J. A. T. *Redating the New Testament.* Philadelphia: Westminster, 1976.

Rorsch, F. "Revelation as 'Subversive Literature.'" *BDV* 54 (2000): 13–15.

Rose, H. J. *Hygini Fabulae.* 2nd ed. Lugduni Batavorum: A. W. Sythoff, 1963.

Rossing, Barbara R. *The Choice between Two Cities: Whore, Bride, and Empire in the Apocalypse.* Harrisburg, Pa.: Trinity Press International, 1999.

Rostovtzoff, Michael. *The Social and Economic History of the Roman Empire.* Oxford: Clarendon, 1957.

Royalty, Robert. *The Streets of Heaven: The Ideology of Wealth in the Apocalypse of John.* Macon, Ga.: Mercer University Press, 1998.

Schreiber, Stephan. *Gesalbter und König: Titel und Konzeptionen der königlichen Gesalbternerwartung in früjudischen und urchristlichen Schriften.* Berlin: de Gruyter, 2000.

Schüssler Fiorenza, Elizabeth. *The Book of Revelation: Justice and Judgment.* Minneapolis: Fortress Press, 1998.

———. *Revelation: Vision of a Just World.* Minneapolis: Fortress Press, 1991.

Screiber, Theodore. *Apollon Pythoktonos: Ein Betrag zur griechischen Religions- und Kunstgeschichte.* Leipzig: Engelmann, 1879.

Shea, William H. "The Parallel Literary Structure of Revelation 12 and 20." *AUSS* 23 (1985): 37–54.

Shelton, Jo Ann. *As the Romans Did: A Sourcebook in Roman Social History.* 2nd ed. New York: Oxford University Press, 1998.

Smallwood, E. Mary. *The Jews under Roman Rule: From Pompey to Diocletian.* Leiden: Brill, 1976.

Smith, Jonathan Z. "Cross-Cultural References on Apocalypticism." Pages 281–5 in *Ancient and Modern Perspectives on the Bible and Culture: Essays in Honor of Hans Dieter Betz.* Edited by Adela Yarbro Collins. Atlanta: Scholars, 1998.

Spitta, Friedrich. *Die Offenbarung de Johannes.* Halle a. S.: Waisenhaus, 1889.

Theissen, Gerd, and Annette Merz. *The Historical Jesus: A Comprehensive Guide.* Minneapolis: Fortress Press, 1996.

———. *Jesus als historische Gestalt: Bëitrage zur Jesusforschung.* Göttingen: Vandenhoeck & Ruprecht, 2003.

Thompson, Leonard L. *The Book of Revelation: Apocalypse and Empire.* New York: Oxford University Press, 1990.

Touron del Pie, Eliseo. "Interpretacion Mariana del Capitulo XII del Apocalipsis en Los Commentarios Barrocas del Siglo XVII." *Estudios* 41:148 (1985): 81–91.

Trebilco, Paul R. *Jewish Communities in Asia Minor.* Cambridge: Cambridge University Press, 1991.

Unger, D. J. "Did Saint John See the Virgin Mary in Glory? (Apoc. 12:1)." *CBQ* 11 (1949): 249–62, 392–405; 12 (1950): 75–83, 155–61, 292–300, 405–15.

Van Henten, Jan Willem. "Dragon Myth and Imperial Ideology in Revelation 12–13." Pages 496–515 in *SBL Seminar Papers* 130 (1994).

Vermeule, C. C. *Roman Imperial Art in Greece and Asia Minor.* Cambridge, Mass.: Harvard University Press, 1968.

Vischer, Eberhard. *Die Offenbarung Johannis: Eine jüdische Apokalypse in christlicher Bearbeitung.* TU 2/3. Leipzig: Hinrichs, 1886.

Vischer, G. J. *Omwerkings em Compilatie-Hypothesen toegepast op de Apokalypse van Johannes.* Groningen: Wolters, 1888.

Weber, M. *Ancient Judaism.* New York: Free Press, 1952.

Weiss, Johannes, ed. *Offenbarung des Johannes in die Schriften des Neuen Testaments.* Göttingen: Vandenhoeck & Ruprecht, 1908.

Wellhausen, Julius. *Analyse der Offenbarung Johannis.* AKGWG, N.F. 9/4. Berlin: Weidmann, 1907.

Wengst, Klaus. *Pax Romana and the Peace of Jesus Christ.* Translated by J. Bowden. London: SCM, 1987.

Westcott, B. F. *The Gospel according to Saint John: The Greek Text with Introduction.* London: Murray, 1882.

Worth, R. H. *The Seven Cities of the Apocalypse and Greco-Asian Culture.* New York: Paulist, 1999.

———. *The Seven Cities of the Apocalypse and Roman Culture.* New York: Paulist, 1999.

Wright, Stuart A., ed. *Armageddon in Waco: Critical Perspectives on the Branch Davidian Conflict*. Chicago: University of Chicago Press, 1995.

Yarbro Collins, Adela. *The Apocalypse*. Wilmington: Glazer, 1979.

——. *The Combat Myth in the Book of Revelation*. Missoula, Mont.: Scholars, 1976.

——. *Crisis and Catharsis: The Power of the Apocalypse*. Philadelphia: Westminster, 1984.

——. "Introduction: Early Christian Apocalypticism." *Semeia* 36 (1986): 1–11.

——. "Pergamon in Early Christian Literature." Pages 163–84 in *Pergamon, Citadel of the Gods: Archaeological Record, Literary Description, and Religious Development*. Edited by Helmut Koester. HTS 46. Harrisburg, Pa.: Trinity Press International, 1998.

——. "The Political Perspective of the Revelation of John." *JBL* 96 (1977): 241–2.

Zanker, Paul. *The Power of Images in the Age of Augustus*. Translated by Alan Shapiro. Ann Arbor: University of Michigan Press, 1990.

GUADALUPE AND MEXICAN COLONIAL HISTORY

Beevers, John. *The Sun Her Mantle*. Westminster: Newman, 1953.

Boff, Leonardo. *The Maternal Face of God*. Translated by Robert R. Barr and John Diercksmeier. New York: Harper & Row, 1987.

Brading, D. A. *The First America: The Spanish Monarchy, Creole Patriots and the Liberal State: 1492–1867*. Cambridge: Cambridge University Press, 1991.

——. *Mexican Phoenix: Our Lady of Guadalupe: Image and Tradition across Five Centuries*. Cambridge: Cambridge University Press, 2001.

Brown, Jonathan. *Images and Ideas in Seventeenth Century Spanish Painting*. Princeton: Princeton University Press, 1978.

Brown, Raymond E., et al., eds. *Mary in the New Testament*. Philadelphia: Fortress Press, 1978.

Burkhart, Louise M. *Before Guadalupe: The Virgin Mary in Early Colonial Nahuatl Literature*. Austin: University of Texas Press, 2001.

———. "The Cult of the Virgin of Guadalupe." Pages 198–227 in *South and Meso-American Sprituality: From the Cult of the Feathered Serpent to the Theology of Liberation*. Edited by Gary H. Gossen in collaboration with Miguel León-Portilla. Vol. 4 of *World Spirituality: An Encyclopedic History of the Religious Quest*. New York: Crossroad, 1993.

Campbell, Ena. "The Virgin of Guadalupe and the Female Self-Image: A Mexican Case History." Pages 5–24 in *Mother Worship: Theme and Variations*. Edited by James J. Preston. Chapel Hill: University of North Carolina Press, 1982.

Campos Ponce, Xavier. *La Virgen de Guadalupe y la diosa Tonantzín*. Mexico City: Ediciones JCP CED ISR, 1970.

Casas, Fray Bartolome de las. *In Defense of the Indians*. Translated, edited, and annotated by Stafford Poole, C.M. DeKalb: Northern Illinois University Press, 1974.

———. *A Short Account of the Destruction of the Indies*. London: Penguin, 1992.

———. *The Spanish Colony: London, 1583*. Amsterdam: Theatrum Orbis Terrarum, 1977.

Castillo, Ana, ed. *Goddess of the Americas: Writings on the Virgin of Guadalupe*. New York: Riverhead, 1996.

Cawley, Martinus. *Anthology of Early Guadalupan Literature*. CARA Studies in Popular Devotion 2. Guadalupan Studies 8. Lafayette, Ore.: Guadalupe Abbey, 1984.

Chávez, Fray Angélico. *La Conquistadora: The Autobiography of an Ancient Statue*. Paterson, N.J.: St. Anthony Guild, 1954.

Choquette, Robert, Charles H. Lippy, and Stafford Poole. *Christianity Comes to the Americas: 1492–1776*. New York: Paragon, 1992.

Christian, William A. Jr. *Apparitions in Late Medieval and Renaissance Spain*. Princeton: Princeton University Press, 1981.

———. *Local Religion in Sixteenth Century Spain*. Princeton: Princeton University Press, 1981.

Cortés, Hernán. *Letters from Mexico*. Translated and edited by Anthony Pagden. New Haven: Yale University Press, 1986.

Davis, Richard. *Hakluyt's Voyages*. Boston: Houghton Mifflin, 1981.

Delaney, John J., ed. *A Woman Clothed with the Sun: Eight Great Appearances of Our Lady in Modern Times*. New York: Image, 1961.

Dibble, Charles E. "The Nahuatilization of Christianity." Pages 225–33 in *Sixteenth Century Mexico: The Work of Sahagún*. Edited by Munro S. Edmonson. Albuquerque: University of New Mexico Press, 1974.

Echeagaray, José Ignacio, ed. *Album conmemorativo del 450 aniversario de las apariciones de Nuestra Señora de Guadalupe*. Mexico City: Ediciones Buena Nueva, 1981.

Ecija, P. Diego de. *Libro de la invención de Santa María de Guadalupe*. Edited by Fr. A. Barrado Manzano, OFM. Caceres: Departmento Provincial de Semanarios, 1953.

Ehrling, Bernhard. "Recent Roman Catholic Studies in Mariology." *LQ* (1964): 320–26.

Elizondo, Virgilio. *Guadalupe: Mother of a New Creation*. Maryknoll: Orbis, 1997.

———. *La Morenita: Evangelizer of the Americas*. San Antonio: Mexican American Cultural Center, 1980.

Fuentes, Carlos. *The Buried Mirror: Reflections on Spain and the New World*. New York: Houghton Mifflin, 1992.

Garibay, Angel. "Our Lady of Guadalupe." *New Catholic Encyclopedia* 6:821–2. New York: McGraw-Hill, 1967.

Harrington, Patricia. "Mother of Death, Mother of Rebirth: The Mexican Virgin of Guadalupe." *JAAR* 56/1 (1988): 25–50.

Harris, Max. *Aztecs, Moors, and Christians: Festivals of Reconquest in Mexico and Spain*. Austin: University of Texas Press, 2000.

Huntington, Samuel. *Who Are We? The Challenges of America's National Identity*. New York: Simon & Schuster, 2004.

Kamen, Henry. *Empire: How Spain Became a World Power 1492–1763*. New York: Harper Collins, 2003.

Lafaye, Jacques. *Quetzalcóatl and Guadalupe: The Formation of a Mexican National Conciousness, 1531–1813*. Chicago: University of Chicago Press, 1976.

Laso de la Vega, Luis. *Huei tlamahuiçoltica omonexiti in ilhuicac tlatocacihuapilli Santa Maria totlaçonantzin Guadalupe in nican huey altepenahuac Mexico itocayocan Tepeyacac*. Mexico City: Imprenta de Iuan Ruiz, 1649.

Léon-Portilla, Miguel. *Aztec Thought and Culture*. Translated by Jack Emory Davis. Norman: University of Oklahoma Press, 1963.

————. *The Broken Spears: The Aztec Account of the Conquest of Mexico.* Boston: Beacon, 1962.

————. *Pre-Columbian Literature of Mexico.* Translated by Grace Lobanov and Miguel Léon-Portilla. Norman: University of Oklahoma Press, 1969.

Mann, Charles C. *1491: New Revelations of the Americas before Columbus.* New York: Knopf, 2005.

Marcos, Sylvia, compiler. "Religion and Colonialism: The Impact of Christianity on Indigenous Mesoamerican Beliefs and Practices." Union Seminary (New York) course EC 330, Spring 1998.

Matovina, Timothy. "Guadalupe at Calvary: Patristic Theology in Miguel Sánchez's *Imagen de la Virgen María* (1648)." *TS* 64 (2003): 795–811.

Menocal, María Rosa. *The Arabic Role in Medieval Literary History: A Forgotten Heritage.* Philadelphia: University of Pennsylvania Press, 1987.

————. *Ornament of the World: How Muslims, Jews, and Christians Created a Culture of Tolerance in Medieval Spain.* New York: Little, Brown, 2002.

Meyers, William Starr, ed. *The Mexican War Diary of General B. Chellan.* Vol. 1. Princeton: Princeton University Press, 1917.

Nebel, Richard. *Santa María Tonantzin, Virgen de Guadalupe: Continuidad y transformación religiosa en México.* Mexico City: Fondo de Cultural Económica, 1995.

Paz, Octavio. *Labyrinth of Solitude: Life and Thought in Mexico.* New York: Grove, 1961.

Pelikan, Jaroslav. *Mary through the Centuries: Her Place in Our Culture.* New Haven: Yale University Press, 1996.

Perry, Mary Elizabeth, and Anne J. Cruz, eds. *Cultural Encounters: The Impact of the Inquisition in Spain and the New World.* Berkeley: University of California Press, 1991.

Peterson, Jeannette Favrot. "The Virgin of Guadalupe: Symbol of Conquest or Liberation?" *AJ* (Winter 1992): 39–47.

Phelan, John Leddy. *The Millennial Kingdom of the Franciscans in the New World.* Berkeley: University of California Press, 1970.

Poole, Stafford, C.M. *Our Lady of Guadalupe: The Origins and Sources of a Mexican National Symbol, 1531–1797.* Tucson: University of Arizona Press, 1997.

Poole, Stafford, Lisa Sousa, and James Lockhart, trans. and eds. *The Story of Guadalupe: Luis Laso de la Vega's Huei tlamahuiçoltica of 1649*. Palo Alto: Stanford University Press, 1998.

Portilla, Miguel León. *Aztec Thought and Culture*. Norman: University of Oklahoma Press, 1990.

Rahner, H. *Our Lady and the Church*. Berlin: Regnery, 1966.

Ricard, Robert. *The Spiritual Conquest of Mexico*. Translated by Lesley Byrd Simpson. Berkeley: University of California Press, 1966.

Rodriguez, Jeanette. *Our Lady of Guadalupe: Faith and Empowerment among Mexican-American Women*. Austin: University of Texas Press, 1994.

Ruiz, Jean-Pierre. "The Bible and U.S. Hispanic American Theological Discourse: Lessons from a Non-Innocent History." Pages 100–20 in *From the Heart of Our People: Latino/a Explorations in Catholic Systematic Theology*. Edited by Orlando O. Espín and Miguel H. Díaz. Maryknoll: Orbis, 1999.

———. "Taking a Stand on the Sand of the Seashore: A Postcolonial Exploration of Revelation 13." Pages 119–35 in *Reading the Book of Revelation: A Resource for Students*. Edited by David L. Barr. Atlanta: Society of Biblical Literature, 2003.

Sahagún, Bernardino de. *Florentine Codex: General History of the Things of New Spain*. Translated with annotations by Arthur J. O. Anderson and Charles E. Dibble. Santa Fe, N.M.: School of American Research and the University of Utah, 1958.

———. *Historia general de las cosas de Nueva España*. 3 vols. Mexico City: Ed. Carlos Maria de Bustamante, 1829–30.

———. *A History of Ancient Mexico*. Vol. 1. Translated by Fanny R. Bandelier. Nashville: Fisk University Press, 1932.

Sánchez, Miguel. *Imagen de la Virgen María Madre de Dios de Guadalupe* (1648). In *Testimonios históricos guadalupanos*. Ed. Ernesto de la Torre Villar and Ramiro Navarro de Anda. Mexico City: Fondo de Cultura Económica, 1982, 152–281.

Siller-Acuña, Clodomiro L. *Flor y canto del Tepeyac: Historia de las apariciones de Sta. Maria; Texto y comentario*. Xalapa, Veracruz: Servir, 1981.

Smith, Jody Brant. *The Image of Guadalupe, Myth or Miracle.* New York: Doubleday, 1984.

Sousa, Lisa, Stafford Poole, C.M and James Lockhart, trans. and eds. *The Story of Guadalupe: Luis Laso de la Vega's Huie tlamahuiçoltica 1649.* Palo Alto: Stanford University Press, 1998.

Todorov, Tzvetan. *The Conquest of America: The Question of the Other.* New York: Harper & Row, 1987.

Warner, Marina. *Alone of All Her Sex: The Myth and the Cult of the Virgin Mary.* New York: Knopf, 1976.

Watson, Simone. *The Cult of Our lady of Guadalupe: A Historical Study.* Collegeville, Minn.: Liturgical Press, 1964.

Wolf, Eric. "The Virgin of Guadalupe: A Mexican National Symbol." Pages 226–30 in *Reader in Comparative Religion: An Anthropological Approach.* Edited by William A. Lessa and Evon Z. Vogt. New York: Harper & Row, 1968.

CHICANA/O STUDIES AND U.S. HISTORY

Acuña, Rodolfo. *Anything but Mexican: Chicanos in Contemporary Los Angeles.* New York: Verso, 1997.

———. *Occupied America: A History of Chicanos.* Pearson Education, 1999.

Anzaldua, Gloria. *Borderlands/La Frontera: The New Mestiza.* San Francisco: Aunt Lute, 1999.

Brinkley, Alan. *American History: A Survey.* 2 vols. 9th ed. New York: McGraw-Hill, 1995.

Burke, John Francis. *Mestizo Democracy: The Politics of Crossing Borders.* College Station: Texas A&M University Press, 2002.

Burns, Edward McNall. *The American Idea of Mission: Concepts of National Purpose and Destiny.* New Brunswick: Rutgers University Press, 1957.

Calderon, Hector, et al., eds. *Criticism in the Borderlands: Studies in Chicano Literature, Culture, and Ideology.* Durham, N.C.: Duke University Press, 1991.

Chamberlain, Samuel E. *My Confessions.* New York: Harper & Row, 1956.

Cockcroft, Eva Sperling, and Holly Barnet-Sánchez, eds. *Signs from the Heart: California Chicano Murals.* Albuquerque: University of New Mexico Press, 1993.

Córdova, Teresa. *Chicano Studies: Critical Connection between Research and Community.* Albuquerque: National Association for Chicano Studies, 1992.

Du Bois, W. E. B. *The Souls of Black Folk.* New York: Bantam, 1989.

Espin, Orlando. *The Faith of the People: Theological Reflections on Popular Catholicism.* Maryknoll: Orbis, 1997.

Gaspar de Alba, Alicia. *Chicano Art: Inside/outside the Master's House: Cultural Politics and the CARA Exhibition.* Austin: University of Texas Press, 1998.

Goldman, Shifra M. "How, Why, Where, and When It All Happened: Chicano Murals of California." Pages 22–53 in *Signs from the Heart: California Chicano Murals.* Edited by Eva Sperling Cockcroft and Holl Barnet-Sánchez. Albuquerque: University of New Mexico Press (1993).

———. "Mexican Muralism: Its Social-Educative Roles in Latin America and the United States." Pages 281–300 in *The Chicano Studies Reader: An Anthology of Aztlán 1970–2000.* Edited by Eric R. Avila et al. Los Angeles: Chicano Studies Research Center Publications, 2001.

Goldman, Shifra M., and Tomas Ybarra-Frausto. "The Political and Social Contexts of Chicano Art." Pages 83–95 in *CARA: Chicano Art: Resistance and Affirmation.* Edited by Richard Griswold del Castillo, Teresa McKenna, and Yvonne Yarbro-Bejarano. Los Angeles: Wright Art Gallery, UCLA, 1991.

Gonzalez, Justo. *Mañana: Christian Theology from a Hispanic Perspective.* Nashville: Abingdon, 1991.

———. *Out of Every Tribe: Christian Theology at the Ethnic Roundtable.* Nashville: United Methodist Publishing House, 1994.

Graebner, Norman A. *Empire on the Pacific: A Study in American Continental Expansion.* New York: Ronald, 1955.

Griswold del Castillo, Richard. *The Treaty of Guadalupe Hidalgo: A Legacy of Conflict.* Norman: University of Oklahoma Press, 1990.

Griswold del Castillo, Richard, Teresa McKenna, and Yvonne Yarbro-Bejarano, eds. *CARA: Chicano Art: Resistance and Affirmation.* Los Angeles: Wright Art Gallery, UCLA, 1991.

Guerrero, Andrés G. *A Chicano Theology.* Maryknoll: Orbis, 1987.

Haynes, Sam W., and Christopher Morris, eds. *Manifest Destiny and Empire: American Antebellum Expansionism.* College Station: Texas A&M University Press, 1997.

Horsman, Reginal. *Race and Manifest Destiny: The Origins of American Racial Anglo-Saxonism.* Cambridge, Mass.: Harvard University Press, 1981.

Hughes, Richard T. *Myths America Lives By.* Chicago: University of Illinois Press, 2003.

Jewett, Robert. *The Captain America Complex: The Dilemma of Zealous Nationalism.* Philadelphia: Westminster, 1973.

Johanssen, Robert W. "Introduction." Pages 7–20 in *Manifest Destiny and Empire: American Antebellum Expansion.* Edited by Sam W. Haynes and Christopher Morris. College Station: Texas A&M Press, 1997.

Keefe, S., and A. Padilla. *Chicano Identity.* Albuquerque: University of New Mexico Press, 1987.

Krauze, Enrique. *Mexico: A Biography of Power: A History of Modern Mexico, 1810–1996.* New York: Harper, 1998.

Levy, Jacques E. *César Chávez: Autobiography of La Causa.* New York: Norton, 1975.

Lopez, Ian F. Haney. *Racism on Trial: The Chicano Fight for Justice.* Cambridge, Mass.: Harvard University Press, 2003.

McCaffrey, James M. *Army of Manifest Destiny: The American Soldier in the Mexican War: 1846–1848.* New York: New York University Press, 1992.

Meier, Matt S. and Feliciano Rivera. *Dictionary of Mexican American History.* Westport, Conn.: Greenwood, 1981.

Merck, Frederick. *Manifest Destiny and Mission in American History: A Reinterpretation.* New York: Knopf, 1963.

Navarro, Armando. *Mexicano Political Experience in Occupied Aztlán: Struggles and Change.* New York: Alta Mira, 2005.

Noriega, Chon. *Chicanos and Film: Representation and Resistance.* Minneapolis: University of Minnesota Press, 1992.

———. *The Chicano Studies Reader: An Anthology of Aztlán.* Los Angeles: UCLA Chicano Studies Research Center, 2001.

Paredes, Américo. *"With His Pistol in His Hand": A Border Ballad and Its Hero.* Austin: University of Texas Press, 1958.

Pattison, Mark. *Isaac Casaubon: 1559–1614.* 2nd ed. Oxford: Clarendon Press, 1892.

Pérez-Torres, Rafael. "Reconfiguring Aztlán." Pages 213–39 in *The Chicano Studies Reader: An Anthology of Aztlán 1970–2000.* Edited by Eric R. Avila et al. Los Angeles: Chicano Studies Research Center, 2001.

Pina, Michael. "The Archaic, Historical and Mythicized Dimensions of Aztlán." Pages 14–48 in *Aztlán: Essays on the Chicano Homeland.* Edited by Rudolfo Anaya and Francisco Lomeli. Albuquerque: Academia/El Norte, 1989.

Rendón, Armando B. *Chicano Manifesto.* New York: Collier, 1970.

Rochfurt, Desmond. *Mexican Muralists.* San Francisco: Chronicle, 1993.

Rochin, Refugio I., and Dennis N. Valdés. *Voices of a New Chicana/o History.* East Lansing: Michigan State University Press, 2002.

Rosales, F. Arturo. *Chicano: The History of the Mexican American Civil Rights Movement.* Houston: Arte Público, 1996.

Salazar, Ruben. "Who Is a Chicano? And What Is It that Chicanos Want?" *Los Angeles Times*, February 6, 1970.

Smith, Jonathan Z. *Drudgery Divine: On the Comparison of Early Christianities and the Religions of Late Antiquity.* Chicago: University of Chicago Press, 1990.

Stevanson, Anders. *Manifest Destiny: American Expansionism and the Empire of Right.* New York: New York University Press, 1995.

Tuveson, Ernest Lee. *Redeemer Nation: The Idea of America's Millennial Role.* Chicago: University of Chicago Press, 1968.

Vélez-Ibañez, Carlos. *Border Visions: Mexican Cultures of the Southwest United States.* Tucson: University of Arizona Press, 1996.

Weinberg, Albert K. *Manifest Destiny: A Study of Nationalist Expansionism in American History.* Baltimore: Johns Hopkins University Press, 1935.

Whitman, Walt. *The Gathering Forces,* I. New York: Putnam's Sons, 1920.

Ybarra-Frausto, Tomas. "Arte Chicano: Images of a Community." Pages 54–67 in *Signs from the Heart: California Chicano Murals*. Eva Sperling Cockcroft and Holly Barnet-Sánchez, eds. Albuquerque: University of New Mexico Press, 1993.

THEORY AND METHODOLOGY

Ahmad, A. *In Theory: Classes, Nations, Literatures*. London: Verso, 1992.

Aldama, Arturo J., and Naomi H. Quiñonez, eds. *Decolonial Voices: Chicana and Chicano Cultural Studies in the 21st Century*. Bloomington: Indiana University Press, 2002.

Aronna, Michael, et al., eds. *The Postmodernism Debate in Latin America*. Durham, N.C.: Duke University Press, 1995.

Arteaga, Alfred. *Chicano Poetics: Heterotexts and Hybridities*. Cambridge: Cambridge University Press, 1997.

Ashcroft, Bill, Gareth Griffins, and Hellen Tiffins. *The Empire Writes Back: Theory and Practice in Post-Colonial Literatures*. New York: Routledge, 2002.

———, eds. *The Post-Colonial Studies Reader*. London: Routledge, 1995.

———, eds. *Post-Colonial Studies: The Key Concepts*. New York: Routledge, 1998.

Atkinson, Donald R., George Morton, and David Sue. *Counseling American Minorities: A Cross Cultural Perspective*. Dubuque, Iowa: Brown, 1979.

Bachrach, P., and M. S. Baratz. *Power and Poverty: Theory and Practice*. New York: Oxford University Press, 1970.

Bakhtin, M. *The Dialogic Imagination: Four Essays*. Edited by Michael Holquist. Austin: University of Texas Press, 1981.

Barker, Francis, Peter Hulme, and Margaret Iverson, eds. *Colonial Discourse/Postcolonial Theory*. New York: Manchester University Press, 1994.

Beverley, John. *Subalternity and Representation: Arguments in Cultural Theory*. Durham, United Kingdom: Durham University Press, 1999.

Bhabha, Homi K. *The Location of Culture*. New York: Routledge, 1994.

Billington, Ray A., and James B. Hedges. *Westward Expansion: A History of the American Frontier*. New York: Macmillan, 1949.

Blount, Brian K. *Cultural Interpretation: Reorienting New Testament Criticism.* Minneapolis: Fortress Press, 1995.

Bourdieu, Pierre. *Algeria 1960.* Cambridge: Cambridge University Press, 1969.

———. *Outline of a Theory of Practice.* Cambridge: Cambridge University Press, 1997.

Bourdieu, Pierre, and Loïc J. D. Wacquont. *An Invitation to Reflexive Sociology.* Chicago: University of Chicago Press, 1992.

Childs, Peter, and Patrick Williams. *An Introduction to Post-Colonial Theory.* London: Prentice-Hall, 1997.

Chrisman, Laura, and Patrick Williams, eds. *Colonial Discourse/Post-Colonial Theory: A Reader.* New York: Columbia University Press, 1994.

Comaroff, Jean. *Body of Power, Spirit of Resistance: The Culture and History of a South African People.* Chicago: University of Chicago Press, 1985.

Coombes, Annie E. "The Recalcitrant Object: Cultural Contact and the Question of Hybridity." Pages 89–114 in *Colonial Discourse/Postcolonial Theory.* Edited by Francis Barker, Peter Hulme, and Margaret Iverson. Manchester: Manchester University Press, 1994.

Crossley, Nick. *Key Concepts in Critical Social Theory.* London: Sage, 2005.

Dussel, Enrique. "Eurocentrism and Modernity (Introduction to the Frankfurt Lectures)." Pages 65–76 in *The Postmodern Debate in Latin America.* Edited by Michael Aronna, John Beverley, and José Oviedo. Durham, N.C.: Duke University Press, 1995.

Fannon, Franz. *Black Skins, White Masks.* New York: Grove, 1991.

Freire, Paulo. *Pedagogy of the Oppressed.* New York: Continuum, 2003.

Geertz, Clifford. "Art as a Cultural System." *MLN* 91 (1976): 1473–99.

Gundaker, Grey. *Signs of Diaspora, Diaspora of Signs: Literacies, Creolization, and Vernacular Practice.* New York: Oxford University Press, 1998.

Harlow, Barbara. *Resistance Literature.* New York: Methuen, 1987.

Hinds, Stephen. *Allusion and Intertext: Dynamics of Appropriation in Roman Poetry.* New York: Cambridge University Press, 1998.

Kautsky, John H. *The Politics of Aristocratic Empires*. Chapel Hill: University of North Carolina Press, 1982.

Lazarus, Neil, ed. *The Cambridge Companion to Postcolonial Literary Studies*. Cambridge: Cambridge University Press, 2004.

Mignolo, Walter D. *Local Histories/Global Designs: Coloniality, Subaltern Knowledges, and Border Thinking*. Princeton: Princeton University Press, 2000.

Parry, B. "Problems in Current Discourse Theory." *OLR* 9 (1994): 27–58.

Ricoeur, Paul. *Interpretation Theory: Discourse and the Surplus of Meanings*. Fort Worth: Texas Christian University Press, 1976.

Said, Edward W. *Culture and Imperialism*. New York: Random House, 1994.

———. *Orientalism*. New York: Vintage, 1979.

———. *The World, the Text, and the Critic*. Cambridge, Mass.: Harvard University Press, 1983.

Schreiter, Robert. *Constructing Local Theologies*. Maryknoll: Orbis, 1985.

Schüssler Fiorenza, Elisabeth. *Rhetoric and Ethic: The Politics of Biblical Studies*. Minneapolis: Fortress Press, 1999.

Scott, James C. *Weapons of the Weak: Everyday Forms of Peasant Resistance*. New Haven: Yale University Press, 1985.

———. *Domination and the Arts of Resistance: Hidden Transcripts*. New Haven: Yale University Press, 1990.

Segovia, Fernando F. *Decolonizing Biblical Studies: A View from the Margins*. Maryknoll: Orbis, 2000.

———. "Interpreting beyond Borders: Postcolonial Studies and Diasporic Studies in Biblical Criticism." Pages 11–34 in *Interpreting beyond Borders*. Edited by Fernando F. Segovia. The Bible and Colonialism 3. Sheffield: Sheffield Academic, 2000.

———. "Reading the Bible Ideologically: Socioeconomic Criticism." *To Each Its Own Meaning: An Introduction to Biblical Criticisms and Their Applications*. Edited by Steven L. McKenzie and Stephen R. Haynes. Louisville: Westminster John Knox, 1999.

Segovia, Fernando F., and Mary Ann Tolbert. *Readings from This Place: Social Location and Biblical Interpretation in the United States*. Minneapolis: Fortress Press, 1995.

Smith, Andrew. "Migrancy, Hybridity, and Postcolonial Literary Studies." *The Cambridge Companion to Postcolonial Literary Studies*. Edited by Neil Lazarus. Cambridge: Cambridge University Press, 2004.

Smith, Theophus H. *Conjuring Culture: Biblical Formations of Black America*. Oxford: Oxford University Press, 1994.

Smith, Wilfred Cantwell. *What Is Scripture? A Comparative Approach*. Minneapolis: Fortress Press, 1993.

Smith-Christopher, Daniel, ed. *Text and Experience: Towards a Cultural Exegesis of the Bible*. Biblical Seminar 35. Sheffield: Sheffield Academic, 1995.

Spivak, Gayatri. "Can the Subaltern Speak?" Pages 277–313 in *Marxism and the Interpretation of Culture*. Edited by Cary Nelson and Lawrence Grossberg. Urbana: University of Illinois Press, 1988.

Sugirtharajah, R. S. *The Bible and the Third World: Precolonial, Colonial and Postcolonial Encounters*. Cambridge: Cambridge University Press, 2001.

———, ed. *The Postcolonial Bible*. Sheffield: Sheffield Academic, 1998.

———. *Postcolonial Criticism and Biblical Interpretation*. Oxford University Press, 2002.

———. *Voices from the Margin: Interpreting the Bible in the Third World*. Maryknoll: Orbis, 1995.

Turner, Victor. *Dramas, Fields and Metaphors: Symbolic Action in Human Society*. Ithaca, N.Y.: Cornell University Press, 1974.

Wimbush, Vincent L., ed. *African Americans and the Bible: Sacred Texts and Social Textures*. New York: Continuum, 2000.

———. "Contemptus Mundi Means . . . 'Bound for the Promised Land': Religion from the Site of Cultural Marronage," in *Papers of the Henry Luce III Fellows in Theology* 2. Edited by J. Strom. Atlanta, Ga.: Scholars, 134.

———. "Introduction: Interpreting Resistance, Resisting Interpretations." *Semeia* (1997): 1–10.

Young, R. J. C. *Colonial Desire: Hybridity in Theory, Culture and Race*. London: Routledge, 1995.

INDEX

Acuña, Rodolfo, 89, 91, 94–95
Alurista, 101–4
ambivalence, 8–9, 119
Antony, Marc, 19–20, 21, 30
Apocalysm, 50–52
Apollo. See *under* Dragon Slayer
myth
art. *See* Chicana/o art
Augustus. *See* Octavian
Aune, David E., 33
Aztecs, 57–59, 61, 103
Aztlán, 58, 102–4, 109, 129, 182
n. 1
*See also Plan Espiritual de
Aztlán, El*

Barklay, John, 30
Barnet-Sánchez, Holly, 107
Bhabha, Homi, 115–16, 118–19,
121
Bible, 25–26, 39, 42, 51, 121,
124–25
biblical criticism, 6–8, 121,
123–26
Daniel 26–27, 39
Psalm 2:9, 33
Revelations 35–37, 168 n. 78
Revelations XII, 2, 5, 11, 14,
22–25, 32, 35, 39–45, 71
Billington, Ray, 89
Boring, Eugene, 21
Botello, Paul, 146

Brading, D.A., 162
Brown Berets, 100–101, 178 n. 50
Burkhart, Louise, 75
Bustamante, Francisco de, 63–65

Cabrera, Armando, 142
Castillo, Griswold del, 100
Chamberlain, Samuel, 90
chaos. *See under* Dragon Slayer
myth
Charlesworth, James, 25
Chávez, César, 2, 97–98, 101,
108–10, 179 n. 67
Chicana/o, 1, 94–113
activists, 101–5, 112
entymology, 94–95
stereotypes, 95–96, 112
Chicana/o art, 1, 105
and cultural identity, 105–13,
116
inspriration for, 106–7
and Mexican art, 106–8
as performance, 1, 105
as sociopolitical resistance, 1,
106–7, 111
as subversion, 111
See also muralism *under*
Virgin of Guadalupe myth
Christian communities
in Asia Minor, 34, 45
conflict with Gentiles, 36–37
conflict with Jews, 35–36, 39